Bastiat's *The Law*

Bastiat's *The Law*

The Institute of Economic Affairs

First published in Great Britain in 2001 by
The Institute of Economic Affairs
2 Lord North Street
Westminster
London SW1P 3LB
in association with Profile Books Ltd

Reprinted 2009

The mission of the Institute of Economic Affairs is to improve public
understanding of the fundamental institutions of a free society, by analysing
and expounding the role of markets in solving economic and social problems.

A CIP catalogue record for this book is available from the British Library.

ISBN-10: 0 255 36509 8
ISBN-13: 978 0 255 36509 3

Many IEA publications are translated into languages other than English or are
reprinted. Permission to translate or to reprint should be sought from the
Director General at the address above.

Typeset in Stone by MacGuru Ltd
info@macguru.org.uk

Printed and bound in Great Britain by Hobbs the Printers

CONTENTS

FOREWORD

Claude Frédéric Bastiat was born in Bayonne on 30 June 1801 and died in 1850. To celebrate the 200th anniversary of his birth, the Institute is reprinting one of his best-known works, *The Law*, first published in the year of his death, with a new introduction by Professor Norman Barry of the University of Buckingham.

Bastiat was a convinced and articulate free trader, having been influenced by Richard Cobden's Anti-Corn Law League. He was firmly in the French laissez-faire tradition, noted for his exposure of economic fallacies (which abounded in nineteenth-century France, as they do today). His writings were characterised by sharp wit and an unusual ability to communicate complicated ideas. Indeed, Joseph Schumpeter described him as 'the most brilliant economic journalist who ever lived'.[1]

In Professor Barry's words, Bastiat 'anticipated many of the insights of public choice theory, demonstrated the superiority of decisions by the impersonal market ... produced intellectually brilliant ... arguments on behalf of free trade ... and provided arguments against socialism that are still relevant'. At the same time, Bastiat recognised the importance of the law and morality. He was

---

1 See *The New Palgrave: A Dictionary of Economics*, John Eatwell, Murray Milgate and Peter Newman (eds), Macmillan, 1987, Volume 1, pp. 204–5, for the quotation from Schumpeter, a list of Bastiat's other works and comments on his contribution to economics.

concerned that government was using the 'law' to become too active a participant in the economy and was devoting too little attention to protecting life and liberty. His ideas have obvious application to the present day as governments encroach more and more on the lives of citizens by passing laws and implementing regulations.

As in all IEA publications, the views expressed are those of the authors, not those of the Institute (which has no corporate view), its managing trustees, Academic Advisory Council members or senior staff. The version of *The Law* which is published here is reproduced by kind permission of the Foundation for Economic Education, Irvington-on-Hudson, New York, which originally published it in 1998 in a translation from the French by Dean Russell.

COLIN ROBINSON

Editorial Director, Institute of Economic Affairs
Professor of Economics, University of Surrey
December 2001

INTRODUCTION

Frédéric Bastiat (1801–50)

As we celebrate the 200th anniversary of the birth of Frédéric Bastiat we should remember that France once had a vibrant tradition of market economics. While it is true that Marxist social philosophy has dominated French intellectual life for at least the past fifty years, and even today a form of interventionism resists the allure of Anglo-American individualism, early in the nineteenth century the French theoretical *laissez-faire* tradition defended a form of the market more efficaciously than did the English classical school (from Adam Smith to Ricardo). Friedrich Hayek somewhat traduced this legacy when, in a famous essay,[1] he claimed that the whole of the French intellectual tradition was infected with a form of rationalism which rejected the market explanation of spontaneous order. But historically the English classical school had degenerated under the influence of Ricardo. He had assumed that the free market was inherently vulnerable to certain necessary processes: rising population would drive down wages to subsistence, the returns to capital would fall and income would be increasingly absorbed by land rent in the 'stationary state'. In this

---

1   F. A. Hayek, 'Individualism: True and False' in *Individualism and Economic Order*, London, Routledge and Kegan Paul, 1948, pp. 1–32. Hayek was, of course, familiar with Bastiat's work and wrote an introduction to a book quoted below.

class theory of society, workers, capitalists and landowners were engaged in a struggle for returns. In this rigid, deterministic model there is no room for the entrepreneur, the fecundity of the market and the creative powers of the *free* individual.

But the French market theorists were different. Already Jean Baptiste Say had discovered the entrepreneur and distinguished his return (profit) from that of the capitalist, who simply earned interest from his investment. And it was the entrepreneur who used the creative powers of individual liberty to drive the market process towards new discoveries and fresh opportunities for profit. Bastiat took up these ideas and demonstrated the fundamental harmony produced by the exchange process. While Bastiat's ventures into *pure* theory, for example in the explanation of value and in the defence of land rent,[2] were either misleading or plain wrong, his informal arguments for the market and private property were formidable. He anticipated many of the insights of public choice theory, demonstrated the superiority of decisions by the impersonal market as against politics (he recognised from an early stage that politicians do not represent the public interest but only that of a coalition of rent-seeking interest groups), produced intellectually brilliant, as well as witty, arguments on behalf of free trade (in which he was a close collaborator of Richard Cobden who was instrumental in the repeal of the Corn Laws in 1846) and provided arguments against socialism that are still relevant to today's

---

2   Bastiat had no concept of the margin and subjective utility and still thought of value in terms of the exchange of labour services. Furthermore, his idea that land rent represented justified earnings of owners who brought it into use was a gift for followers of Henry George, who plausibly claimed that rent was an unjustified payment to the lucky owners who made no contribution to production. It could be taxed away with no loss in efficiency.

still statist world. In a sentence of stunning clarity yet profound intelligence, he famously declared that the 'state is that fictitious institution by which everybody tries to live at the expense of everybody else'.[3]

But his arguments for the market are nested comfortably in a highly plausible theory of law and morality. Towards the end of his life he seemed to have lost the battle for free trade in France and his country had been afflicted with various forms of socialistic experimentation in 1848.[4] Bastiat spent the last few years of his life producing articles and tracts against the new collectivist menace. But he knew that economics was not enough; that the theory of a free society needed an account of law, a theory of legitimate property and a proper explanation of the limits of government. He knew on utilitarian grounds that socialism does not work, but he wanted to show that collectivism was destructive of freedom, human dignity and the proper moral constraints that should govern human action. The result of his labours was *The Law*.

This work, written while Bastiat was dying of tuberculosis, was published as a pamphlet in June 1850. It elaborated the moral ideas already implicit in his economic work and constitutes his main contribution to political theory. He noticed quite early in his literary career that the legal system had developed some deleterious features during the nineteenth century. The law had become an instrument of politics, not the handmaiden of freedom.

---

3   See his essay 'The State' in *Selected Essays on Political Economy*, edited by George B. de Huszar, Irvington-on-Hudson, Foundation for Economic Education, 1995, p. 144.

4   For an historical account of the events of 1848, see Dean Russell, *Frédéric Bastiat: Ideas and Influence*, Irvington-on-Hudson, Foundation for Economic Education, 1965.

Accordingly, he wrote: 'The law is no longer the refuge of the oppressed, but the arm of the oppressor. The law is no longer a shield but a sword.'[5] Bastiat argued that government, using the 'law', had become an active participant in the economy, and in so doing had stopped protecting life, liberty and free exchange. It had become merely an instrument of *power*, and hence it was in danger of losing the respect that it should have in a civilised society. It had ceased to be a system of impartial and general rules, which individuals need for stability and predictability in an uncertain world, but was becoming the 'legal' embodiment of a series of arbitrary decrees issued by governments in pursuit of collective plans. Of course, the situation has become much worse today and Bastiat's analysis of proper legal processes has a resonance that applies universally. The problem that exercised Bastiat was that modern governments were using the dignity and ethical status that we attach to the word law for purposes that were antithetical to the correct understanding of legality, which must be derived from an objective, individualistic ethic.

It is important to stress, then, that Bastiat was no legal positivist, prepared to use the word law for any formally valid utterance of a legislative assembly. In his view, the law had to fulfil certain moral criteria if it were to be used correctly. The main features of that morality which Bastiat stressed were liberty, justice and property. Law understood in the context of morality was a harmonious whole, as self-consistent and as self-correcting as the parts in an economic system. Consistent with this natural law doctrine is the claim that positive law does not create property and that liberty is not a gift of the legislature. Both are intrinsic

---

5 'Plunder and the Law', in *Selected Essays on Political Economy*, p. 235.

features of human action that is free from coercion. Freedom is being left alone, subject to the constraint that it is impermissible to undermine the equal rights of others. If the positive law enforces this then the harmony is complete: law is justice. It is all derived from an accurate account of *man*: 'Life, faculties, production ... this is man. And in spite of the cunning of artful political leaders, these three gifts from God precede all human legislation and are superior to it.'[6]

The powers of the positive law are morally limited to the powers of each individual. Law is the collective organisation for the individual right of self-defence and it cannot possess, or perform, what individuals cannot possess or perform. Although Bastiat declared the aims of the socialists are inconsistent with economic science, he recognised that these goals were actually more likely to come about if legislators simply left the market to itself. Natural competition would produce equality, as workers moved automatically to more productive, higher-paying occupations and in the long run rates of interest would be identical as capital moved to the most propitious venues. Whatever inequality remained after competition merely reflects the different productivity of labour, and is 'eternally just'.[7] But law and justice are understood negatively: 'Justice is achieved only when injustice is absent.'[8] In the modern world, 'social justice', or some arbitrarily determined level of income, has become the aim of legislators. For Bastiat, this was not merely inefficient; it was immoral.

The law becomes perverted when the state takes on things outside its permissible range of activity. Bastiat seemed aware that

---

6   *The Law*, pp. 21–2 of this edition.

7   'Property and Plunder', in *Selected Essays on Political Economy*, p. 180.

8   *The Law*, p. 43.

there is so little agreement about the content of an expanded notion of justice that only dissent and disharmony will follow the state's attempt to implement the socially just society. The same applies to that other concept of the French Revolution, fraternity. Apart from the natural reciprocity and automatic sociability that arise from friendship and market exchange, the concept has no descriptive features. According to Bastiat, socialist politicians merely seized the idea of fraternity and enforced it on people. But compulsory cooperation is no cooperation at all: it is forced conformity.

While Bastiat was a firm believer in natural rights,[9] he was disturbed that the extension of the law into inappropriate areas introduced a new concept of acquired rights, which distorted the basic idea of rights. Acquired rights arise from the expansion of government rather than from the natural moral relationships between individuals. Under this new concept the right to work no longer meant the prohibition of man-made impediments to the search for jobs, but rather the artificial creation of non-economic employment by government. As well as making no economic sense, such ventures attenuated the clarity and determinacy of genuine rights claims. One can imagine Bastiat's reaction to the endless manufacture of social and economic rights by democratic governments today. He would have been the first to notice that the multiplication of rights claims reduces their value (the ambitious morality of modern democratic politics cannot repeal the laws of economics). Rights should be negative, as is justice. It was a feature of the socialist agitation of 1848 that the traditional language of liberal politics was perverted and twisted towards collectivist ends by people like Louis Blanc.

---

9   *The Law*, p. 35.

Behind the distortion of the meaning of modern law, Bastiat detected the influence of the ancient classical tradition with its anti-individualism and implicit totalitarianism. In *The Law* he paid special attention to Mably, one of the most sinister of the extreme republicans of the Revolution. Mably's open identification of virtue with terror was not only a kind of moral licence for the infliction of cruelty and suffering, but it also represented a complete reversal of traditional ways of moral thinking.[10] Ethical principles are no longer rules and conventions that expand our liberty and enable us to exchange in peace; they are now the instruments of dictatorship. Men are being forced to die for an idea that emanates exclusively from the head of the Legislator.

Although he regularly voted with the Left in the Assembly, Bastiat was never a party man. He always voted according to his conscience. The fact that this sometimes placed him on the same side of an issue as the socialists was due to the practical reality that there were enough moral issues on which he could agree with them. Characteristically, when his bitter economic enemy Louis Blanc was tried by the Assembly for conspiracy and insurrection against the state, Bastiat defended him and voted for his acquittal. A thorough examination of the evidence convinced him that the charges against Blanc were groundless. Bastiat also voted in 1849 against proposed laws to prohibit labour unions; they were part of the backlash against the working-class excesses of the previous year. Bastiat's belief in the principle of liberty impelled him to support the right not to work. There was, however, a tactical explanation for his actions. He did not want the government to be blamed for any unemployment. He knew perfectly well that

---

10   *The Law*, p. 66.

unions cannot raise pay above (marginal) productivity, but he did not want the public to be deceived about the true causes of low pay and unemployment. If workers' organisations were banned, that action itself would be held to be the cause of any distress.

Despite his voting record, Bastiat never departed from his economic principles. He insisted that socialism was legalised plunder, that it could not possibly work and that it would be the antithesis of the free society. To the end he insisted on the conceptual link between freedom and property.[11] When the state takes someone's possessions the crime is not exhausted by their removal but also by denial of the moral agency of the victim. In a sense, the identity of the person is established by his property, by which Bastiat meant property *in* the person. One's natural abilities are as much a part of his property as one's physical goods. In this respect Bastiat followed principles espoused by John Locke. And at one level it is certainly true, for if a person did not possess property in his own skills and capacities, he could not exercise his economic liberty; he could not, for example, be an entrepreneur. For indisputable utilitarian reasons one can easily demonstrate the futility of high taxation and other types of government-inspired plunder, but Bastiat wanted to go further than this: he wanted to place property and freedom firmly in the tradition of western morality. While we have earlier expressed some doubts about the morality of exclusive land ownership, in all other respects Bastiat's defence of property clearly resonates with modern libertarianism.

At his death, much of what Bastiat had fought for throughout his life seemed threatened. The free-trade movement in France was virtually finished (though there was some belated and diluted

---

11   *The Law*, pp. 40–46.

recognition of his work in the Anglo-French commercial treaty of 1860) and various forms of collectivism seemed to have a grip on the French psyche. The optimistic free-market movement to which he belonged withered as the country embarked on a clear collectivist course that prospered as time went on. It is thriving today. It is true that his cohort, Gustave de Molinari, took up his ideas and developed them in an anarcho-capitalist direction, but Molinari had little impact on the course of events, and is virtually unknown today outside specialist circles.

Despite the events of history, Bastiat's legacy is impressive and lasting. His arguments provide formidable artillery in any contemporary attack on statism. His legacy has special relevance in his native France. Riddled by enormously costly welfare, ruinously high taxation and an open contempt for the free-market capitalism of the Anglo-American tradition, which is now going through something of a minor revival, contemporary France would drive Bastiat to despair. Although most French intellectuals have given up on outright collectivism, a form of European 'capitalism' has developed which would have provoked Bastiat's scorn. One can imagine Bastiat's mordant response to the recent French government's imposition of a maximum 35-hour working week, justified on the grounds that it would save jobs. 'Why not ten hours?' he would probably have said. 'Think how many jobs that would save.'

Bastiat's ideas are also capable of extension. One issue that would have excited him is the possibility of going beyond the market for regular goods and services and exploring the idea of competitive jurisdictions. People do often migrate to areas where taxation and regulation are less oppressive. In the modern, global economy the costs of exit are lower than they were even ten years ago. However, the European Union with its desire to centralise and regulate internationally is rapidly reducing the possibility of such competition. The politicians who run the Union are the world's most assiduous rent-seekers and they know perfectly well that jurisdictional competition would severely reduce these rents. That is why a stream of regulations and directives from Brussels has systematically expunged variety and competition from European nations. What is the point in emigrating if the laws are much the same wherever you go? It is a situation that would have enraged Bastiat, but I am sure he would have relished the intellectual combat it provokes. And the truly impressive thing about *The Law* is that it is a book whose central message can be used in a variety of different circumstances. Because it deals with both economics and politics its fundamental principles have a timeless quality about them.

NORMAN BARRY

Professor of Politics, University of Buckingham

December 2001

The Law

THE LAW

The law perverted! And the police powers of the state perverted along with it! The law, I say, not only turned from its proper purpose but made to follow an entirely contrary purpose! The law become the weapon of every kind of greed! Instead of checking crime, the law itself is guilty of the evils it is supposed to punish!

If this is true, it is a serious fact, and moral duty requires me to call the attention of my fellow-citizens to it.

Life is a gift from God

We hold from God the gift which includes all others. This gift is life – physical, intellectual, and moral life.

But life cannot maintain itself alone. The Creator of life has entrusted us with the responsibility of preserving, developing, and perfecting it. In order that we may accomplish this, He has provided us with a collection of marvellous faculties. And He has put us in the midst of a variety of natural resources. By the application of our faculties to these natural resources we convert them into products, and use them. This process is necessary in order that life may run its appointed course.

Life, faculties, production – in other words, individuality, liberty, property – this is man. And in spite of the cunning of artful political leaders, these three gifts from God precede all human legislation, and are superior to it.

Life, liberty, and property do not exist because men have made laws. On the contrary, it was the fact that life, liberty, and property existed beforehand that caused men to make laws in the first place.

What is law?

What, then, is law? It is the collective organisation of the individual right to lawful defence.

Each of us has a natural right – from God – to defend his person, his liberty, and his property. These are the three basic requirements of life, and the preservation of any one of them is completely dependent upon the preservation of the other two. For what are our faculties but the extension of our individuality? And what is property but an extension of our faculties?

If every person has the right to defend – even by force – his person, his liberty, and his property, then it follows that a group of men have the right to organise and support a common force to protect these rights constantly. Thus the principle of collective right – its reason for existing, its lawfulness – is based on individual right. And the common force that protects this collective right cannot logically have any other purpose or any other mission than that for which it acts as a substitute. Thus, since an individual cannot lawfully use force against the person, liberty, or property of another individual, then the common force – for the same reason – cannot lawfully be used to destroy the person, liberty, or property of individuals or groups.

Such a perversion of force would be, in both cases, contrary to our premise. Force has been given to us to defend our own individual rights. Who will dare to say that force has been given to us to destroy the equal rights of our brothers? Since no individual acting separately can lawfully use force to destroy the rights of others, does it not logically follow that the same principle also applies to the common force that is nothing more than the organised combination of the individual forces?

If this is true, then nothing can be more evident than this: the law is the organisation of the natural right of lawful defence. It is the substitution of a common force for individual forces. And this common force is to do only what the individual forces have a natural and lawful right to do: to protect persons, liberties, and properties; to maintain the right of each, and to cause *justice* to reign over us all.

A just and enduring government

If a nation were founded on this basis, it seems to me that order would prevail among the people, in thought as well as in deed. It seems to me that such a nation would have the most simple, easy to accept, economical, limited, non-oppressive, just, and enduring government imaginable – whatever its political form might be.

Under such an administration, everyone would understand that he possessed all the privileges as well as all the responsibilities of his existence. No one would have any argument with government, provided that his person was respected, his labour was free, and the fruits of his labour were protected against all unjust attack. When successful, we would not have to thank the state for our success. And, conversely, when unsuccessful, we would no more think of blaming the state for our misfortune than would the farmers blame the state because of hail or frost. The state would be felt only by the invaluable blessings of safety provided by this concept of government.

It can be further stated that, thanks to the non-intervention of the state in private affairs, our wants and their satisfactions would develop themselves in a logical manner. We would not see poor families seeking literary instruction before they have bread. We would not see cities populated at the expense of rural districts, nor rural districts at the expense of cities. We would not see the great displacements of capital, labour, and population that are caused by legislative decisions.

The sources of our existence are made uncertain and precarious by these state-created displacements. And, furthermore, these acts burden the government with increased responsibilities.

The complete perversion of the law

But, unfortunately, law by no means confines itself to its proper functions. And when it has exceeded its proper functions, it has not done so merely in some inconsequential and debatable matters. The law has gone further than this; it has acted in direct opposition to its own purpose. The law has been used to destroy its own objective: it has been applied to annihilating the justice that it was supposed to maintain; to limiting and destroying rights which its real purpose was to respect. The law has placed the collective force at the disposal of the unscrupulous who wish, without risk, to exploit the person, liberty, and property of others. It has converted plunder into a right, in order to protect plunder. And it has converted lawful defence into a crime, in order to punish lawful defence.

How has this perversion of the law been accomplished? And what have been the results?

The law has been perverted by the influence of two entirely

different causes: stupid greed and false philanthropy. Let us speak of the first.

A fatal tendency of mankind

Self-preservation and self-development are common aspirations among all people. And if everyone enjoyed the unrestricted use of his faculties and the free disposition of the fruits of his labour, social progress would be ceaseless, uninterrupted, and unfailing.

But there is also another tendency that is common among people. When they can, they wish to live and prosper at the expense of others. This is no rash accusation. Nor does it come from a gloomy and uncharitable spirit. The annals of history bear witness to the truth of it: the incessant wars, mass migrations, religious persecutions, universal slavery, dishonesty in commerce, and monopolies. This fatal desire has its origin in the very nature of man – in that primitive, universal, and insuppressible instinct that impels him to satisfy his desires with the least possible pain.

Property and plunder

Man can live and satisfy his wants only by ceaseless labour; by the ceaseless application of his faculties to natural resources. This process is the origin of property.

But it is also true that a man may live and satisfy his wants by seizing and consuming the products of the labour of others. This process is the origin of plunder.

Now since man is naturally inclined to avoid pain – and since labour is pain in itself – it follows that men will resort to plunder whenever plunder is easier than work. History shows this quite clearly. And under these conditions, neither religion nor morality can stop it.

When, then, does plunder stop? It stops when it becomes more painful and more dangerous than labour. It is evident, then, that the proper purpose of law is to use the power of its collective force to stop this fatal tendency to plunder instead of to work. All the measures of the law should protect property and punish plunder.

But, generally, the law is made by one man or one class of men. And since law cannot operate without the sanction and support of a dominating force, this force must be entrusted to those who make the laws.

This fact, combined with the fatal tendency that exists in the heart of man to satisfy his wants with the least possible effort, explains the almost universal perversion of the law. Thus it is easy to understand how law, instead of checking injustice, becomes the invincible weapon of injustice. It is easy to understand why the law is used by the legislator to destroy in varying degrees among the rest of the people their personal independence by slavery, their liberty by oppression, and their property by plunder. This is done for the benefit of the person who makes the law, and in proportion to the power that he holds.

Victims of lawful plunder

Men naturally rebel against the injustice of which they are victims. Thus, when plunder is organised by law for the profit of those who make the law, all the plundered classes try somehow to enter – by peaceful or revolutionary means – into the making of laws. According to their degree of enlightenment, these plundered classes may propose one of two entirely different purposes when they attempt to attain political power: either they may wish to stop lawful plunder, or they may wish to share in it.

Woe to the nation when this latter purpose prevails among the mass victims of lawful plunder when they, in turn, seize the power to make laws!

Until that happens, the few practise lawful plunder upon the many, a common practice where the right to participate in the making of law is limited to a few persons. But then, participation in the making of law becomes universal. And then, men seek to balance their conflicting interests by universal plunder. Instead of rooting out the injustices found in society, they make these injustices general. As soon as the plundered classes gain political power, they establish a system of reprisals against other classes. They do not abolish legal plunder. (This objective would demand more enlightenment than they possess.) Instead, they emulate their evil predecessors by participating in this legal plunder, even though it is against their own interests.

It is as if it were necessary, before a reign of justice appears, for everyone to suffer a cruel retribution – some for their evilness, and some for their lack of understanding.

The results of legal plunder

It is impossible to introduce into society a greater change and a greater evil than this: the conversion of the law into an instrument of plunder.

What are the consequences of such a perversion? It would require volumes to describe them all. Thus we must content ourselves with pointing out the most striking.

In the first place, it erases from everyone's conscience the distinction between justice and injustice.

No society can exist unless the laws are respected to a certain degree. The safest way to make laws respected is to make them respectable. When law and morality contradict each other, the citizen has the cruel alternative of either losing his moral sense or losing his respect for the law. These two evils are of equal consequence, and it would be difficult for a person to choose between them.

The nature of law is to maintain justice. This is so much the case that, in the minds of the people, law and justice are one and the same thing. There is in all of us a strong disposition to believe that anything lawful is also legitimate. This belief is so widespread that many persons have erroneously held that things are – just – because law makes them so. Thus, in order to make plunder appear just and sacred to many consciences, it is only necessary for the law to decree and sanction it. Slavery, restrictions, and monopoly find defenders not only among those who profit from them but also among those who suffer from them.

The fate of non-conformists

If you suggest a doubt as to the morality of these institutions, it is boldly said that 'You are a dangerous innovator, a utopian, a theorist, a subversive; you would shatter the foundation upon which society rests.'

If you lecture upon morality or upon political science, there will be found official organisations petitioning the government in this vein of thought: 'That science no longer be taught exclusively from the point of view of free trade (of liberty, of property, and of justice) as has been the case until now, but also, in the future, science is to be especially taught from the viewpoint of the facts and laws that regulate French industry (facts and laws which are contrary to liberty, to property, and to justice). That, in government-endowed teaching positions, the professor rigorously refrain from endangering in the slightest degree the respect due to the laws now in force.'[1]

Thus, if there exists a law which sanctions slavery or monopoly, oppression or robbery, in any form whatever, it must not ever be mentioned. For how can it be mentioned without damaging the respect which it inspires? Still further, morality and political economy must be taught from the point of view of this law; from the supposition that it must be a just law merely because it is a law.

Another effect of this tragic perversion of the law is that it gives an exaggerated importance to political passions and conflicts, and to politics in general.

I could prove this assertion in a thousand ways. But, by way of illustration, I shall limit myself to a subject that has lately occupied the minds of everyone: universal suffrage.

Who shall judge?

The followers of Rousseau's school of thought – who consider themselves far advanced, but whom I consider twenty centuries behind the times – will not agree with me on this. But universal suffrage – using the word in its strictest sense – is not one of those sacred dogmas which it is a crime to examine or doubt. In fact, serious objections may be made to universal suffrage.

---

1   General Council of Manufacturers, Agriculture, and Commerce, 6 May 1850.

In the first place, the word *universal* conceals a gross fallacy. For example, there are 36 million people in France. Thus, to make the right of suffrage universal, there should be 36 million voters. But the most extended system permits only 9 million people to vote. Three persons out of four are excluded. And more than this, they are excluded by the fourth. This fourth person advances the principle of *incapacity* as his reason for excluding the others. Universal suffrage means, then, universal suffrage for those who are capable. But there remains this question of fact: who is capable? Are minors, females, insane persons, and persons who have committed certain major crimes the only ones to be determined incapable?

The reason why voting is restricted

A closer examination of the subject shows us the motive which causes the right of suffrage to be based upon the supposition of incapacity. The motive is that the elector or voter does not exercise this right for himself alone, but for everybody.

The most extended elective system and the most restricted elective system are alike in this respect. They differ only in respect to what constitutes incapacity. It is not a difference of principle, but merely a difference of degree.

If, as the republicans of our present-day Greek and Roman schools of thought pretend, the right of suffrage arrives with one's birth, it would be an injustice for adults to prevent women and children from voting. Why are they prevented? Because they are presumed to be incapable. And why is incapacity a motive for exclusion? Because it is not the voter alone who suffers the consequences of his vote; because each vote touches and affects everyone in the entire community; because the people in the community have a right to demand some safeguards concerning the acts upon which their welfare and existence depend.

The answer is to restrict the law

I know what might be said in answer to this; what the objections might be. But this is not the place to exhaust a controversy of this nature. I wish merely to observe here that this controversy over universal suffrage (as well as most other political questions) which agitates, excites, and overthrows nations would lose nearly all of its importance if the law had always been what it ought to be.

In fact, if law were restricted to protecting all persons, all liberties, and all properties; if law were nothing more than the organised combination of the individual's right to self defence; if law were the obstacle, the check, the punisher of all oppression and plunder – is it likely that we citizens would then argue much about the extent of the franchise?

Under these circumstances, is it likely that the extent of the right to vote would endanger that supreme good, the public peace? Is it likely that the excluded classes would refuse to peaceably await the coming of their right to vote? Is it likely that those who had the right to vote would jealously defend their privilege?

If the law were confined to its proper functions, everyone's interest in the law would be the same. Is it not clear that, under these circumstances, those who voted could not inconvenience those who did not vote?

The fatal idea of legal plunder

But on the other hand, imagine that this fatal principle has been introduced: under the pretence of organisation, regulation, protection, or encouragement, the law takes property from one person and gives it to another; the law takes the wealth of all and gives it to a few – whether farmers, manufacturers, shipowners, artists, or comedians. Under these circumstances, then certainly every class will aspire to grasp the law, and logically so.

The excluded classes will furiously demand their right to vote – and will overthrow society rather than not to obtain it. Even beggars and vagabonds will then prove to you that they also have an incontestable title to vote. They will say to you:

'We cannot buy wine, tobacco, or salt without paying the tax. And a part of the tax that we pay is given by law – in privileges and subsidies – to men who are richer than we are. Others use the law to raise the prices of bread, meat, iron, or cloth. Thus, since everyone else uses the law for his own profit, we also would like to use the law for our own profit. We demand from the law the *right to relief*, which is the poor man's plunder. To obtain this right, we also should be voters and legislators in order that we may organise Beggary on a grand scale for our own class, as you have organised Protection on a grand scale for your class. Now don't tell us beggars that you will act for us, and then toss us, as Mr Mimerel proposes, 600,000 francs to keep us quiet, like throwing us a bone to gnaw. We have other claims. And anyway, we wish to bargain for ourselves as other classes have bargained for themselves!'

And what can you say to answer that argument!

Perverted law causes conflict

As long as it is admitted that the law may be diverted from its true purpose – that it may violate property instead of protecting it – then everyone will want to participate in making the law, either to protect himself against plunder or to use it for plunder. Political questions will always be prejudicial, dominant, and all-absorbing. There will be fighting at the door of the Legislative Palace, and the struggle within will be no less furious. To know this, it is hardly necessary to examine what transpires in the French and English legislatures; merely to understand the issue is to know the answer.

Is there any need to offer proof that this odious perversion of the law is a perpetual source of hatred and discord; that it tends to destroy society itself? If such proof is needed, look at the United States [in 1850]. There is no country in the world where the law is kept more within its proper domain: the protection of every person's liberty and property. As a consequence of this, there appears to be no country in the world where the social order rests on a firmer foundation. But even in the United States, there are two issues – and only two – that have always endangered the public peace.

Slavery and tariffs are plunder

What are these two issues? They are slavery and tariffs. These are the only two issues where, contrary to the general spirit of the republic of the United States, law has assumed the character of a plunderer.

Slavery is a violation, by law, of liberty. The protective tariff is a violation, by law, of property.

It is a most remarkable fact that this double *legal crime* – a sorrowful inheritance from the Old World – should be the only issue which can, and perhaps will, lead to the ruin of the Union. It is indeed impossible to imagine, at the very heart of a society, a more astounding fact than this: *the law has come to be an instrument of injustice.* And if this fact brings terrible consequences to the United States – where the proper purpose of the law has been perverted only in the instances of slavery and tariffs – what must be the consequences in Europe, where the perversion of the law is a principle; a system?

Two kinds of plunder

Mr de Montalembert [politician and writer], adopting the thought contained in a famous proclamation by Mr Carlier, has said: 'We must make war against socialism.' According to the definition of socialism advanced by Mr Charles Dupin, he meant: 'We must make war against plunder.'

But of what plunder was he speaking? For there are two kinds of plunder: legal and illegal.

I do not think that illegal plunder, such as theft or swindling – which the penal code defines, anticipates, and punishes – can be called socialism. It is not this kind of plunder that systematically threatens the foundations of society. Anyway, the war against this kind of plunder has not waited for the command of these gentlemen. The war against illegal plunder has been fought since the beginning of the world. Long before the Revolution of February 1848 – long before the appearance even of socialism itself – France had provided police, judges, gendarmes, prisons, dungeons, and scaffolds for the purpose of fighting illegal plunder. The law itself conducts this war, and it is my wish and opinion that the law should always maintain this attitude towards plunder.

The law defends plunder

But it does not always do this. Sometimes the law defends plunder and participates in it. Thus the beneficiaries are spared the shame, danger, and scruple which their acts would otherwise involve. Sometimes the law places the whole apparatus of judges, police, prisons, and gendarmes at the service of the plunderers, and treats the victim when he defends himself as a criminal. In short, there is a legal plunder, and it is of this, no doubt, that Mr de Montalembert speaks.

This legal plunder may be only an isolated stain among the legislative measures of the people. If so, it is best to wipe it out with a minimum of speeches and denunciations – and in spite of the uproar of the vested interests.

How to identify legal plunder

But how is this legal plunder to be identified? Quite simply. See if the law takes from some persons what belongs to them, and gives it to other persons to whom it does not belong. See if the law benefits one citizen at the expense of another by doing what the citizen himself cannot do without committing a crime.

Then abolish this law without delay, for it is not only an evil itself, but also it is a fertile source for further evils because it invites reprisals. If such a law – which may be an isolated case – is not abolished immediately, it will spread, multiply, and develop into a system.

The person who profits from this law will complain bitterly, defending his *acquired rights*. He will claim that the state is obligated to protect and encourage his particular industry; that this procedure enriches the state because the protected industry is thus able to spend more and to pay higher wages to the poor working men.

Do not listen to this sophistry by vested interests. The acceptance of these arguments will build legal plunder into a whole system. In fact, this has already occurred. The present-day delusion is an attempt to enrich everyone at the expense of everyone else; to make plunder universal under the pretence of organising it.

Legal plunder has many names

Now, legal plunder can be committed in an infinite number of ways. Thus we have an infinite number of plans for organising it: tariffs, protection, benefits, subsidies, encouragements, progressive taxation, public schools, guaranteed jobs, guaranteed profits, minimum wages, a right to relief, a right to the tools of labour, free credit, and so on, and so on. All these plans as a whole – with their common aim of legal plunder – constitute socialism.

Now, since under this definition socialism is a body of doctrine, what attack can be made against it other than a war of doctrine? If you find this socialistic doctrine to be false, absurd, and evil, then refute it. And the more false, the more absurd, and the more evil it is, the easier it will be to refute. Above all, if you wish to be strong, begin by rooting out every particle of socialism that may have crept into your legislation. This will be no light task.

Socialism is legal plunder

Mr de Montalembert has been accused of desiring to fight socialism by the use of brute force. He ought to be exonerated from this accusation, for he has plainly said: 'The war that we must fight against socialism must be in harmony with law, honour, and justice.'

But why does not Mr de Montalembert see that he has placed himself in a vicious circle? You would use the law to oppose socialism? But it is upon the law that socialism itself relies. Socialists desire to practice *legal* plunder, not *illegal* plunder. Socialists, like all other monopolists, desire to make the law their own weapon. And when once the law is on the side of socialism, how can it be used against socialism? For when plunder is abetted by the law, it does not fear your courts, your gendarmes, and your prisons. Rather, it may call upon them for help.

To prevent this, you would exclude socialism from entering into the making of laws? You would prevent socialists from entering the Legislative Palace? You shall not succeed, I predict, so long as legal plunder continues to be the main business of the legislature. It is illogical – in fact, absurd – to assume otherwise.

The choice before us

This question of legal plunder must be settled once and for all, and there are only three ways to settle it:

1 The few plunder the many.
2 Everybody plunders everybody.
3 Nobody plunders anybody.

We must make our choice among limited plunder, universal plunder, and no plunder. The law can follow only one of these three.

Limited legal plunder

This system prevailed when the right to vote was restricted. One would turn back to this system to prevent the invasion of socialism.

Universal legal plunder

We have been threatened with this system since the franchise was made universal. The newly enfranchised majority has decided to formulate law on the same principle of legal plunder that was used by their predecessors when the vote was limited.

No legal plunder

This is the principle of justice, peace, order, stability, harmony, and logic. Until the day of my death, I shall proclaim this principle with all the force of my lungs (which alas! is all too inadequate).[2]

The proper function of the law

And, in all sincerity, can anything more than the absence of plunder be required of the law? Can the law – which necessarily requires the use of force – rationally be used for anything except protecting the rights of everyone? I defy anyone to extend it beyond this purpose without perverting it and, consequently, turning might against right. This is the most fatal and most illogical social perversion that can possibly be imagined. It must

---

[2] Translator's note: at the time this was written, Mr Bastiat knew that he was dying of tuberculosis. Within a year, he was dead.

be admitted that the true solution – so long searched for in the area of social relationships – is contained in these simple words: *law is organised justice*.

Now this must be said: when justice is organised by law – that is, by force – this excludes the idea of using law (force) to organise any human activity whatever, whether it be labour, charity, agriculture, commerce, industry, education, art, or religion. The organising by law of any one of these would inevitably destroy the essential organisation – justice. For truly, how can we imagine force being used against the liberty of citizens without it also being used against justice, and thus acting against its proper purpose?

The seductive lure of socialism

Here I encounter the most popular fallacy of our times. It is not considered sufficient that the law should be just; it must be philanthropic. Nor is it sufficient that the law should guarantee to every citizen the free and inoffensive use of his faculties for physical, intellectual, and moral self-improvement. Instead, it is demanded that the law should directly extend welfare, education, and morality throughout the nation.

This is the seductive lure of socialism. And I repeat again: these two uses of the law are in direct contradiction to each other. We must choose between them. A citizen cannot at the same time be free and not free.

Enforced fraternity destroys liberty

Mr de Lamartine once wrote to me thus: 'Your doctrine is only the half of my programme. You have stopped at liberty; I go on to fraternity.' I answered him: 'The second half of your programme will destroy the first.'

In fact, it is impossible for me to separate the word *fraternity* from the word *voluntary*. I cannot possibly understand how fraternity can be *legally* enforced without liberty being *legally* destroyed, and thus justice being *legally* trampled underfoot.

Legal plunder has two roots: one of them, as I have said before, is in human greed; the other is in false philanthropy.

At this point, I think that I should explain exactly what I mean by the word *plunder*.[3]

Plunder violates ownership

I do not, as is often done, use the word in any vague, uncertain, approximate, or metaphorical sense. I use it in its scientific acceptance – as expressing the idea opposite to that of property [wages, land, money, or whatever]. When a portion of wealth is transferred from the person who owns it – without his consent and without compensation, and whether by force or by fraud – to anyone who does not own it, then I say that property is violated; that an act of plunder is committed.

I say that this act is exactly what the law is supposed to suppress, always and everywhere. When the law itself commits this act that it is supposed to suppress, I say that plunder is still committed, and I add that from the point of view of society and welfare, this aggression against rights is even worse. In this case of legal plunder, however, the person who receives the benefits is not responsible for the act of plundering. The responsibility for this

---

3   Translator's note: the French word used by Mr Bastiat is *spoliation*.

legal plunder rests with the law, the legislator, and society itself. Therein lies the political danger.

It is to be regretted that the word *plunder* is offensive. I have tried in vain to find an inoffensive word, for I would not at any time – especially now – wish to add an irritating word to our dissentions. Thus, whether I am believed or not, I declare that I do not mean to attack the intentions or the morality of anyone. Rather, I am attacking an *idea* which I believe to be false; a *system* which appears to me to be unjust; an injustice so independent of personal intentions that each of us profits from it without wishing to do so, and suffers from it without knowing the cause of the suffering.

Three systems of plunder

The sincerity of those who advocate protectionism, socialism, and communism is not here questioned. Any writer who would do that must be influenced by a political spirit or a political fear. It is to be pointed out, however, that protectionism, socialism, and communism are basically the same plant in three different stages of its growth. All that can be said is that legal plunder is more visible in communism because it is complete plunder; and in protectionism because the plunder is limited to specific groups and industries.[4] Thus it follows that, of the three systems, socialism is the vaguest,

---

4   If the special privilege of government protection against competition – monopoly – were granted only to one group in France, the iron workers, for instance, this act would so obviously be legal plunder that it could not last for long. It is for this reason that we see all the protected trades combined into a common cause. They even organise themselves in such a manner as to appear to represent all persons who labour. Instinctively, they feel that legal plunder is concealed by generalising it.

the most indecisive, and, consequently, the most sincere stage of development.

But sincere or insincere, the intentions of persons are not here under question. In fact, I have already said that legal plunder is based partially on philanthropy, even though it is a false philanthropy.

With this explanation, let us examine the value – the origin and the tendency – of this popular aspiration which claims to accomplish the general welfare by general plunder.

Law is force

Since the law organises justice, the socialists ask why the law should not also organise labour, education, and religion.

Why should not law be used for these purposes? Because it could not organise labour, education, and religion without destroying justice. We must remember that law is force, and that, consequently, the proper functions of the law cannot lawfully extend beyond the proper functions of force.

When law and force keep a person within the bounds of justice, they impose nothing but a mere negation. They oblige him only to abstain from harming others. They violate neither his personality, his liberty, nor his property. They safeguard all of these. They are *defensive*; they defend equally the rights of all.

Law is a negative concept

The harmlessness of the mission performed by law and lawful defence is self-evident; the usefulness is obvious; and the legitimacy cannot be disputed.

As a friend of mine once remarked, this negative concept of law is so true that the statement *the purpose of the law is to cause justice to reign* is not a rigorously accurate statement. It ought to be stated that *the purpose of the law is to prevent injustice from reigning*. In fact, it is injustice, instead of justice, that has an existence of its own. Justice is achieved only when injustice is absent.

But when the law, by means of its necessary agent, force, imposes upon men a regulation of labour, a method or a subject of education, a religious faith or creed – then the law is no longer negative; it acts positively upon people. It substitutes the will of the legislator for their own wills; the initiative of the legislator for their own initiatives. When this happens, the people no longer need to discuss, to compare, to plan ahead; the law does all this for them. Intelligence becomes a useless prop for the people; they cease to be men; they lose their personality, their liberty, their property.

Try to imagine a regulation of labour imposed by force that is not a violation of liberty; a transfer of wealth imposed by force that is not a violation of property. If you cannot reconcile these contradictions, then you must conclude that the law cannot organise labour and industry without organising injustice.

The political approach

When a politician views society from the seclusion of his office, he is struck by the spectacle of the inequality that he sees. He deplores the deprivations which are the lot of so many of our brothers, deprivations which appear to be even sadder when contrasted with luxury and wealth.

Perhaps the politician should ask himself whether this state of affairs has not been caused by old conquests and lootings, and by more recent legal plunder. Perhaps he should consider this proposition: since all persons seek well-being and perfection, would not a condition of justice be sufficient to cause the greatest efforts toward progress, and the greatest possible equality that is compatible with individual responsibility? Would not this be in accord with the concept of individual responsibility which God has willed in order that mankind may have the choice between vice and virtue, and the resulting punishment and reward?

But the politician never gives this a thought. His mind turns to organisations, combinations, and arrangements – legal or apparently legal. He attempts to remedy the evil by increasing and perpetuating the very thing that caused the evil in the first place: legal plunder. We have seen that justice is a negative concept. Is there even one of these positive legal actions that does not contain the principle of plunder?

The law and charity

You say: 'There are persons who have no money,' and you turn to the law. But the law is not a breast that fills itself with milk. Nor are the lacteal veins of the law supplied with milk from a source outside the society. Nothing can enter the public treasury for the benefit of one citizen or one class unless other citizens and other classes have been *forced* to send it in. If every person draws from the treasury the amount that he has put in it, it is true that the law then plunders nobody. But this procedure does nothing for the persons who have no money. It does not promote equality of income. The law can be an instrument of equalisation only as it takes from some persons and gives to other persons. When the law does this, it is an instrument of plunder.

With this in mind, examine the protective tariffs, subsidies, guaranteed profits, guaranteed jobs, relief and welfare schemes, public education, progressive taxation, free credit, and public works. You will find that they are always based on legal plunder, organised injustice.

The law and education

You say: 'There are persons who lack education' and you turn to the law. But the law is not, in itself, a torch of learning which shines its light abroad. The law extends over a society where some persons have knowledge and others do not; where some citizens need to learn, and others can teach. In this matter of education, the law has only two alternatives: it can permit this transaction of teaching-and-learning to operate freely and without the use of force, or it can force human wills in this matter by taking from some of them enough to pay the teachers who are appointed by government to instruct others, without charge. But in this second case, the law commits legal plunder by violating liberty and property.

The law and morals

You say: 'Here are persons who are lacking in morality or religion,' and you turn to the law. But law is force. And need I point out what a violent and futile effort it is to use force in the matters of morality and religion?

It would seem that socialists, however self-complacent, could not avoid seeing this monstrous legal plunder that results from such systems and such efforts. But what do the socialists do? They cleverly disguise this legal plunder from others – and even from themselves – under the seductive names of fraternity, unity, organisation, and association. Because we ask so little from the law – only justice – the socialists thereby assume that we reject fraternity, unity, organisation, and association. The socialists brand us with the name *individualist*.

But we assure the socialists that we repudiate only *forced* organisation, not natural organisation. We repudiate the forms of association that are *forced* upon us, not free association. We repudiate *forced* fraternity, not true fraternity. We repudiate the *artificial* unity that does nothing more than deprive persons of individual responsibility. We do not repudiate the natural unity of mankind under Providence.

A confusion of terms

Socialism, like the ancient ideas from which it springs, confuses the distinction between government and society. As a result of this, every time we object to a thing being done by government, the socialists conclude that we object to its being done at all.

We disapprove of state education. Then the socialists say that we are opposed to any education. We object to a state religion. Then the socialists say that we want no religion at all. We object to a state-enforced equality. Then they say that we are against equality. And so on, and so on. It is as if the socialists were to accuse us of not wanting persons to eat because we do not want the state to raise grain.

The influence of socialist writers

How did politicians ever come to believe this weird idea that the law could be made to produce what it does not contain – the wealth, science, and religion that, in a positive sense, constitute prosperity? Is it due to the influence of our modern writers on public affairs?

Present-day writers – especially those of the socialist school of thought – base their various theories upon one common hypothesis: they divide mankind into two parts. People in general – with the exception of the writer himself – form the first group. The writer, all alone, forms the second and most important group. Surely this is the weirdest and most conceited notion that ever entered a human brain!

In fact, these writers on public affairs begin by supposing that people have within themselves no means of discernment; no motivation to action. The writers assume that people are inert matter, passive particles, motionless atoms, at best a kind of vegetation indifferent to its own manner of existence. They assume that people are susceptible to being shaped – by the will and hand of another person – into an infinite variety of forms, more or less symmetrical, artistic, and perfected.

Moreover, not one of these writers on governmental affairs hesitates to imagine that he himself – under the title of organiser, discoverer, legislator, or founder – is this will and hand, this universal motivating force, this creative power whose sublime mission is to mould these scattered materials – persons – into a society.

These socialist writers look upon people in the same manner that the gardener views his trees. Just as the gardener capriciously shapes the trees into pyramids, parasols, cubes, vases, fans, and other forms, just so does the socialist writer whimsically shape human beings into groups, series, centres, sub-centres, honeycombs, labour-corps, and other variations. And just as the gardener needs axes, pruning hooks, saws, and shears to shape his trees, just so does the socialist writer need the force that he can find only in law to shape human beings. For this purpose, he devises tariff laws, tax laws, relief laws, and school laws.

The socialists want to play God

Socialists look upon people as raw material to be formed into social combinations. This is so true that, if by chance, the socialists have any doubts about the success of these combinations, they will demand that a small portion of mankind be set aside *to experiment upon*. The popular idea of *trying all systems* is well known. And one socialist leader has been known seriously to demand that the Constituent Assembly give him a small district with all its inhabitants, to try his experiments upon.

In the same manner, an inventor makes a model before he constructs the full-sized machine; the chemist wastes some chemicals – the farmer wastes some seeds and land – to try out an idea.

But what a difference there is between the gardener and his trees, between the inventor and his machine, between the chemist and his elements, between the farmer and his seeds! And in all sincerity, the socialist thinks that there is the same difference between him and mankind!

It is no wonder that the writers of the nineteenth century look upon society as an artificial creation of the legislator's genius. This idea – the fruit of classical education – has taken possession of all the intellectuals and famous writers of our country. To these intellectuals and writers, the relationship between persons and the legislator appears to be the same as the relationship between the clay and the potter.

Moreover, even where they have consented to recognise a principle of action in the heart of man – and a principle of discernment in man's intellect – they have considered these gifts from God to be fatal gifts. They have thought that persons, under the impulse of these two gifts, would fatally tend to ruin themselves. They assume that if the legislators left persons free to follow their own inclinations, they would arrive at atheism instead of religion, ignorance instead of knowledge, poverty instead of production and exchange.

The socialists despise mankind

According to these writers, it is indeed fortunate that Heaven has bestowed upon certain men – governors and legislators – the exact opposite inclinations, not only for their own sake but also for the sake of the rest of the world! While mankind tends towards evil, the legislators yearn for good; while mankind advances towards darkness, the legislators aspire for enlightenment; while mankind is drawn towards vice, the legislators are attracted towards virtue. Since they have decided that this is the true state of affairs, they then demand the use of force in order to substitute their own inclinations for those of the human race.

Open at random any book on philosophy, politics, or history, and you will probably see how deeply rooted in our country is this idea – the child of classical studies, the mother of socialism. In all of them, you will probably find this idea that mankind is merely inert matter, receiving life, organisation, morality, and prosperity from the power of the state. And even worse, it will be stated that mankind tends towards degeneration, and is stopped from this downward course only by the mysterious hand of the legislator.

Conventional classical thought everywhere says that behind passive society there is a concealed power called *law* or *legislator* (or called by some other terminology that designates some unnamed person or persons of undisputed influence and authority) which moves, controls, benefits, and improves mankind.

A defence of compulsory labour

Let us first consider a quotation from Bossuet [tutor to the Dauphin in the Court of Louis XIV]:

> One of the things most strongly impressed (by whom?) upon the minds of the Egyptians was patriotism . . . No one was permitted to be useless to the state. The law assigned to each one his work, which was handed down from father to son. *No one was permitted* to have two professions. Nor could a person change from one job to another . . . But there was one task to which all were *forced* to conform: the study of the laws and of wisdom. Ignorance of religion and of the political regulations of the country *was not excused* under any circumstances. Moreover each occupation *was assigned* (by whom?) to a certain district . . . Among the good laws, one of the best was that everyone *was trained* (by whom?) to obey them. As a result of this, Egypt was filled with wonderful inventions, and nothing was neglected that could make life easy and quiet.

Thus, according to Bossuet, persons derive nothing from themselves. Patriotism, prosperity, inventions, husbandry, science – all of these are given to the people by the operation of the laws, the rulers. All that the people have to do is to bow to leadership.

A defence of paternal government

Bossuet carries this idea of the state as the source of all progress even so far as to defend the Egyptians against the charge that they rejected wrestling and music. He said:

> How is that possible? These arts were invented by Trismegistus [who was alleged to have been Chancellor to the Egyptian god Osiris].

And again among the Persians, Bossuet claims that all comes from above:

> One of the first responsibilities *of the prince* was to encourage agriculture ... just as there were offices established for the regulation of armies, just so were there offices for the direction of farm work ... The Persian people *were inspired* with an overwhelming respect for royal authority.

And according to Bossuet, the Greek people, although exceedingly intelligent, had no sense of personal responsibility; like dogs and horses, they themselves could not have invented the most simple games:

> The Greeks, naturally intelligent and courageous, *had been early cultivated* by the kings and settlers who had come from Egypt. From these Egyptian rulers, the Greek people had learned bodily exercises, *foot races*, and horse and chariot races ... But the best thing that the Egyptians had taught the Greeks was to become docile, and to permit themselves to be formed by the law for the public good.

The idea of passive mankind

It cannot be disputed that these classical theories [advanced by these latter-day teachers, writers, legislators, economists, and philosophers] held that everything came to the people from a source outside themselves. As another example, take Fenelon [archbishop, author, and instructor to the Duke of Burgundy].

He was a witness to the power of Louis XIV. This, plus the fact that he was nurtured in the classical studies and the admiration of antiquity, naturally caused Fenelon to accept the idea that mankind should be passive; that the misfortunes and the prosperity – vices and virtues – of people are caused by the external influence exercised upon them by the law and the legislators. Thus, in his *Utopia of Salentum*, he puts men – with all their interests, faculties, desires, and possessions – under the absolute discretion of the legislator. Whatever the issue may be, persons do not decide it for themselves; the prince decides for them. The prince is depicted as the *soul* of this shapeless mass of people who form the nation. In the prince resides the thought, the foresight, all progress, and the principle of all organisation. Thus all responsibility rests with him.

The whole of the tenth book of Fenelon's *Telemachus* proves this. I refer the reader to it, and content myself with quoting at random from this celebrated work to which, in every other respect, I am the first to pay homage.

Socialists ignore reason and facts

With the amazing credulity which is typical of the classicists, Fenelon ignores the authority of reason and facts when he attributes the general happiness of the Egyptians, not to their own wisdom but to the wisdom of their kings:

We could not turn our eyes to either shore without seeing rich towns and country estates most agreeably located; fields, never fallowed, covered with golden crops every year; meadows full of flocks; workers bending under the weight of the fruit which the earth lavished upon its cultivators; shepherds who made the echoes resound with the soft notes from their pipes and flutes. 'Happy,' said Mentor, 'is the people governed by a wise king . . .

Later, Mentor desired that I observe the contentment and abundance which covered all Egypt, where twenty-two thousand cities could be counted. He admired the good police regulations in the cities; the justice rendered in favour of the poor *against* the rich; the sound education of the children in obedience, labour, sobriety, and the love of the arts and letters; the exactness with which all religious ceremonies were performed; the unselfishness, the high regard for honour, the faithfulness to men, and the fear of the gods which every father taught his children. He never stopped admiring the prosperity of the country. 'Happy,' said he, 'is the people ruled by a wise king in such a manner.'

Socialists want to regiment people

Fenelon's idyll on Crete is even more alluring. Mentor is made to say:

All that you see in this wonderful island results from the laws of Minos. The education which he ordained for the children makes their bodies strong and robust. From the very beginning, one accustoms the children to a life of frugality and labour, because one assumes that all pleasures of the senses weaken both body and mind. Thus one allows

> them no pleasure except that of becoming invincible by
> virtue, and of acquiring glory ... Here one punishes three
> vices that go unpunished among other people: ingratitude,
> hypocrisy, and greed. There is no need to punish persons for
> pomp and dissipation, for they are unknown in Crete ... No
> costly furniture, no magnificent clothing, no delicious
> feasts, no gilded palaces are permitted.

Thus does Mentor prepare his student to mould and to manipulate – doubtless with the best of intentions – the people of Ithaca. And to convince the student of the wisdom of these ideas, Mentor recites to him the example of Salentum.

It is from this sort of philosophy that we receive our first political ideas! We are taught to treat persons much as an instructor in agriculture teaches farmers to prepare and tend the soil.

A famous name and an evil idea

Now listen to the great Montesquieu on this same subject:

> To maintain the spirit of commerce, it is necessary that all
> the laws must favour it. These laws, by proportionately
> dividing up the fortunes as they are made in commerce,
> should provide every poor citizen with sufficiently easy
> circumstances to enable him to work like the others. These
> same laws should put every rich citizen in such lowered
> circumstances as to force him to work in order to keep or to
> gain.

> Thus the laws are to dispose of all fortunes!

> Although real equality is the soul of the state in a
> democracy, yet this is so difficult to establish that an
> extreme precision in this matter would not always be

desirable. It is sufficient that here be established a census to reduce or fix these differences in wealth within a certain limit. After this is done, it remains for specific laws to equalise inequality by imposing burdens upon the rich and granting relief to the poor.

Here again we find the idea of equalising fortunes by law, by force.

In Greece, there were two kinds of republics. One, Sparta, was military; the other, Athens, was commercial. In the former, *it was desired* that the citizens be idle; in the latter, love of labour *was encouraged*.

Note the marvellous genius of these legislators: by debasing all established customs – by mixing the usual concepts of all virtues – they knew in advance that the world would admire their wisdom.

Lycurgus gave stability to his city of Sparta by combining petty thievery with the soul of justice; by combining the most complete bondage with the most extreme liberty; by combining the most atrocious beliefs with the greatest moderation. He appeared to deprive his city of all its resources, arts, commerce, money, and defences. In Sparta, ambition went without the hope of material reward. Natural affection found no outlet because a man was neither son, husband, nor father. Even chastity was no longer considered becoming. *By this road, Lycurgus led Sparta on to greatness and glory.*

This boldness which was to be found in the institutions of Greece has been repeated in the midst of *the degeneracy and corruption of our modern times*. An occasional honest legislator has moulded a people in whom integrity appears as natural as courage in the Spartans.

Mr William Penn, for example, is a true Lycurgus. Even though Mr Penn had peace as his objective – while Lycurgus had war as his objective – they resemble each other in that their moral prestige over free men allowed them to overcome prejudices, to subdue passions, and to lead *their* respective peoples into new paths.

The country of Paraguay furnishes us with another example [of a people who, for their own good, are moulded by their legislators].[5]

Now it is true that if one considers the sheer pleasure of commanding to be the greatest joy in life, he contemplates a crime against society; it will, however, always be a noble ideal to govern men in a manner that will make them happier.

Those who desire to establish similar institutions must do as follows: establish common ownership of property as in the republic of Plato; revere the gods as Plato commanded; prevent foreigners from mingling with the people, in order to preserve the customs; let the state, instead of the citizens, establish commerce. The legislators should supply arts instead of luxuries; they should satisfy needs instead of desires.

A frightful idea

Those who are subject to vulgar infatuation may exclaim: 'Montesquieu has said this! So it's magnificent! It's sublime!' As for me, I have the courage of my own opinion. I say: what! You have the nerve to call that fine? It is frightful! It is abominable! These random selections from the writings of Montesquieu show that he considers persons, liberties, property – mankind itself – to be nothing but materials for legislators to exercise their wisdom upon.

5   Translator's note: what was then known as Paraguay was a much larger area than it is today. It was colonised by the Jesuits who settled the Indians into villages, and generally saved them from further brutalities by the avid conquerors.

The leader of the democrats

Now let us examine Rousseau on this subject. This writer on public affairs is the supreme authority of the democrats. And although he bases the social structure upon the *will of the people*, he has, to a greater extent than anyone else, completely accepted the theory of the total inertness of mankind in the presence of the legislators:

> If it is true that a great prince is rare, then is it not true that a great legislator is even more rare? The prince has only to follow the pattern that the legislator creates. *The legislator is the mechanic, who invents the machine*; the prince is merely the workman who sets it in motion.

And what part do persons play in all this? They are merely the machine that is set in motion. In fact, are they not merely considered to be the raw material of which the machine is made?

Thus the same relationship exists between the legislator and the prince as exists between the agricultural expert and the farmer; and the relationship between the prince and his subjects is the same as that between the farmer and his land. How high above mankind, then, has this writer on public affairs been placed? Rousseau rules over legislators themselves, and teaches them their trade in these imperious terms:

> Would you give stability to the state? Then bring the extremes as closely together as possible. Tolerate neither wealthy persons nor beggars.
>
> If the soil is poor or barren, or the country too small for its inhabitants, then turn to industry and arts, and trade these products for the foods that you need ... On a fertile soil – if *you are short* of inhabitants – devote all your attention to agriculture, because this multiplies people; *banish* the arts, because they only serve to depopulate the nation ...
>
> If you have extensive and accessible coast lines, then *cover*

the sea with merchant ships; you will have a brilliant but
short existence. If your seas wash only inaccessible cliffs, let
the people *be barbarous* and eat fish; they will live more
quietly – perhaps better – and, most certainly, they will live
more happily.

In short, and in addition to the maxims that are common
to all, every people has its own particular circumstances.
And this fact in itself will cause legislation appropriate to
the circumstances.

This is the reason why the Hebrews formerly – and, more
recently, the *Arabs* – had religion as their principal
objective. The objective of the Athenians was literature; of
Carthage and Tyre, commerce; of Rhodes, naval affairs; of
Sparta, war; and of Rome, virtue. The author of *The Spirit of
Laws* has shown by what art *the legislator should direct his
institutions towards each of these objectives* . . . But suppose
that the legislator mistakes his proper objective, and acts on
a principle different from that indicated by the nature of
things? Suppose that the selected principle sometimes
creates slavery, and sometimes liberty; sometimes wealth,
and sometimes population; sometimes peace, and
sometimes conquest? This confusion of objective will slowly
enfeeble the law and impair the constitution. The state will
be subjected to ceaseless agitations until it is destroyed or
changed, and invincible nature regains her empire.

But if nature is sufficiently invincible to *regain* its empire, why
does not Rousseau admit that it did not need the legislator to *gain*
it in the first place? Why does he not see that men, by obeying their
own instincts, would turn to farming on fertile soil, and to commerce on an extensive and easily accessible coast, without the in-
terference of a Lycurgus or a Solon or a Rousseau *who might easily
be mistaken*.

Socialists want forced conformity

Be that as it may, Rousseau invests the creators, organisers, directors, legislators, and controllers of society with a terrible responsibility. He is, therefore, most exacting with them:

> He who would dare to undertake the political creation of a
> people ought to believe that he can, in a manner of
> speaking, transform human nature; transform each
> individual – who, by himself, is a solitary and perfect whole
> – into a mere part of a greater whole from which the
> individual will henceforth receive his life and being. Thus
> the person who would undertake the political creation of a
> people should believe in his ability to alter man's
> constitution; to strengthen it; to substitute for the physical
> and independent existence received from nature, an
> existence which is partial and moral.[6] In short, the would-be
> creator of political man must remove man's own forces and
> endow him with others that are naturally alien to him.

Poor human nature! What would become of a person's dignity if it were entrusted to the followers of Rousseau?

Legislators desire to mould mankind

Now let us examine Raynal on this subject of mankind being moulded by the legislator:

> The legislator must first consider the climate, the air, and
> the soil. The resources at *his* disposal determine his duties.
> He must first consider *his* locality. A population living on

---

6   Translator's note: according to Rousseau, the existence of social man is partial in
    the sense that he is henceforth merely a part of society – knowing himself as such
    – and thinking and feeling from the point of view of the whole he thereby
    becomes moral.

maritime shores must have laws designed for navigation ...
If it is an inland settlement, the legislator must make his
plans according to the nature and fertility of the soil ...
It is especially in the distribution of property that the genius
of the legislator will be found. As a general rule, when a new
colony is established in any country, sufficient land should
be given to each man to support his family ...

On an uncultivated island that *you* are populating with
children, you need do nothing but let the seeds of truth
germinate along with the development of reason ... But
when *you* resettle a nation with a past into a new country,
the skill of the legislator rests in the policy of *permitting the
people* to retain no injurious opinions and customs which
can possibly be cured and corrected. If *you* desire to prevent
these opinions and customs from becoming permanent, you
will secure the second generation by a general system of
public education for the children. A prince or a legislator
should never establish a colony without first arranging to
send wise men along to instruct the youth ...

In a new colony, ample opportunity is open to the careful
legislator who desires *to purify the customs and manners of the
people*. If he has virtue and genius, the land and the people *at
his disposal* will inspire his soul with a plan for society. A
writer can only vaguely trace the plan in advance because it
is necessarily subject to the instability of all hypotheses; the
problem has many forms, complications, and circumstances
that are difficult to foresee and settle in detail.

Legislators told how to manage men

Raynal's instructions to the legislators on how to manage people
may be compared to a professor of agriculture lecturing his
students: 'The climate is the first rule for the farmer. *His* resources
determine his procedure. He must first consider his locality. If his

soil is clay, he must do so and so. If his soil is sand, he must act in another manner. Every facility is open to the farmer who wishes to clear and improve his soil. If he is skilful enough, the manure *at his disposal* will suggest to him a plan of operation. A professor can only vaguely trace this plan in advance because it is necessarily subject to the instability of all hypotheses; the problem has many forms, complications, and circumstances that are difficult to foresee and settle in detail.'

Oh, sublime writers! Please remember sometimes that this clay, this sand, and this manure which you so arbitrarily dispose of are men! They are your equals! They are intelligent and free human beings like yourselves! As you have, they too have received from God the faculty to observe, to plan ahead, to think, and to judge for themselves!

A temporary dictatorship

Here is Mably on this subject of the law and the legislator. In the passages preceding the one here quoted, Mably has supposed the laws, due to a neglect of security, to be worn out. He continues to address the reader thus:

Under these circumstances, it is obvious that the springs of government are slack. *Give them* a new tension, and the evil will be cured ... Think less of punishing faults, and more of rewarding *that which you need*. In this manner you will restore to *your republic* the vigour of youth. Because free people have been ignorant of this procedure, they have lost their liberty! But if the evil has made such headway that ordinary governmental procedures are unable to cure it, then *resort* to an extraordinary tribunal with considerable powers for a short time. The imagination of the citizens needs to be struck a hard blow.

In this manner, Mably continues through twenty volumes.

Under the influence of teaching like this – which stems from classical education – there came a time when everyone wished to place himself above mankind in order to arrange, organise, and regulate it in his own way.

Socialists want equality of wealth

Next let us examine Condillac on this subject of the legislators and mankind:

> My Lord, assume the character of Lycurgus or of Solon. And before you finish reading this essay, amuse yourself by giving laws to some savages in America or Africa. Confine these nomads to fixed dwellings; teach them to tend flocks . . . Attempt to develop the social consciousness that nature has planted in them . . . Force them to begin to practise the duties of humanity . . . Use punishment to cause sensual pleasures to become distasteful to them. Then you will see that every point of your legislation will cause these savages to lose a vice and gain a virtue.
>
> All people have had laws. But few people have been happy. Why is this so? Because the legislators themselves have almost always been ignorant of the purpose of society, which is the uniting of families by a common interest.
>
> Impartiality in law consists of two things: the establishing of equality in wealth and equality in dignity among the citizens . . . As the laws establish greater equality, they become proportionately more precarious to every citizen . . . When all men are equal in wealth and dignity – and when the laws leave no hope of disturbing this equality – how can

men then be agitated by greed, ambition, dissipation, idleness, sloth, envy, hatred, or jealousy?

What you have learned about the republic of Sparta should enlighten you on this question. No other state has ever had laws more in accord with the order of nature; of equality.

The error of the socialist writers

Actually, it is *not* strange that during the seventeenth and eighteenth centuries the human race was regarded as inert matter, ready to receive everything – form, face, energy, movement, life – from a great prince or great legislator or a great genius. These centuries were nourished on the study of antiquity. And antiquity presents everywhere – in Egypt, Persia, Greece, Rome – the spectacle of a few men moulding mankind according to their whims, thanks to the prestige of force and fraud. But this does not prove that this situation is desirable. It proves only that since men and society are capable of improvement, it is naturally to be expected that error, ignorance, despotism, slavery, and superstition should be greatest towards the origins of history. The writers quoted above were not in error when they found ancient institutions to be such, but they were in error when they offered them for the admiration and imitation of future generations. Uncritical and childish conformists, they took for granted the grandeur, dignity, morality, and happiness of the artificial societies of the ancient world. They did not understand that knowledge appears and grows with the passage of time; and that in proportion to this growth of knowledge, *might* takes the side of *right*, and society regains possession of itself.

What is liberty?

Actually, what is the political struggle that we witness? It is the instinctive struggle of all people towards liberty. And what is this liberty, whose very name makes the heart beat faster and shakes the world? Is it not the union of all liberties – liberty of conscience, of education, of association, of the press, of travel, of labour, of trade? In short, is not liberty the freedom of every person to make full use of his faculties, so long as he does not harm other persons while doing so? Is not liberty the destruction of all despotism – including, of course, legal despotism? Finally, is not liberty the restricting of the law only to its rational sphere of organising the right of the individual to lawful self-defence; of punishing injustice?

It must be admitted that the tendency of the human race towards liberty is largely thwarted, especially in France. This is greatly due to a fatal desire – learned from the teachings of antiquity – that our writers on public affairs have in common: they desire to set themselves above mankind in order to arrange, organise, and regulate it according to their fancy.

Philanthropic tyranny

While society is struggling towards liberty, these famous men who put themselves at its head are filled with the spirit of the seventeenth and eighteenth centuries. They think only of subjecting mankind to the philanthropic tyranny of their own social inventions. Like Rousseau, they desire to force mankind docilely to bear this yoke of the public welfare that they have dreamed up in their own imaginations.

This was especially true in 1789. No sooner was the old regime destroyed than society was subjected to still other artificial arrangements, always starting from the same point: the omnipotence of the law.

Listen to the ideas of a few of the writers and politicians during that period:

SAINT-JUST: The legislator commands the future. It is for him to will the good of mankind. It is for him to make men what he wills them to be.

ROBESPIERRE: The function of government is to direct the physical and moral powers of the nation towards the end for which the commonwealth has come into being.

BILLAUD-VARENNES: A people who are to be returned to liberty must be formed anew. A strong force and vigorous action are necessary to destroy old prejudices, to change old customs, to correct depraved affections, to restrict superfluous wants, and to destroy ingrained vices ... Citizens, the inflexible austerity of Lycurgus created the firm foundation of the Spartan republic. The weak and trusting character of Solon plunged Athens into slavery. This parallel embraces the whole science of government.

LE PELLETIER: Considering the extent of human degradation, I am convinced that it is necessary to effect a total regeneration and, if I may so express myself, of creating a new people.

The socialists want dictatorship

Again, it is claimed that persons are nothing but raw material. It is not for them to *will their own improvement*; they are incapable of it.

According to Saint-Just, only the legislator is capable of doing this. Persons are merely to be what the legislator *wills* them to be. According to Robespierre, who copies Rousseau literally, the legislator begins by decreeing the *end for which the commonwealth has come into being*. Once this is determined, the government has only to direct the *physical and moral forces of the nation* towards that end. Meanwhile, the inhabitants of the nation are to remain completely passive. And according to the teachings of Billaud-Varennes, the people should have no prejudices, no affections, and no desires except those authorised by the legislator. He even goes so far as to say that the inflexible austerity of one man is the foundation of a republic.

In cases where the alleged evil is so great that ordinary governmental procedures cannot cure it, Mably recommends a dictatorship to promote virtue: 'Resort,' he says, 'to an extraordinary tribunal with considerable powers for a short time. The imagination of the citizens needs to be struck a hard blow.' This doctrine has not been forgotten. Listen to Robespierre:

> The principle of the republican government is virtue, and the means required to establish virtue is terror. In our country we desire to substitute morality for selfishness, honesty for honour, principles for customs, duties for manners, the empire of reason for the tyranny of fashion, contempt of vice for contempt of poverty, pride for insolence, greatness of soul for vanity, love of glory for love of money, good people for good companions, merit for intrigue, genius for wit, truth for glitter, the charm of happiness for the boredom of pleasure, the greatness of man for the littleness of the great, a generous, strong, happy people for a good-natured, frivolous, degraded people; in short, we desire to substitute all the virtues and miracles of a republic for all the vices and absurdities of a monarchy.

Dictatorial arrogance

At what a tremendous height above the rest of mankind does Robespierre here place himself! And note the arrogance with which he speaks. He is not content to pray for a great reawakening of the human spirit. Nor does he expect such a result from a well-ordered government. No, he himself will remake mankind, and by means of terror.

This mass of rotten and contradictory statements is extracted from a discourse by Robespierre in which he aims to explain the *principles of morality which ought to guide a revolutionary government*. Note that Robespierre's request for dictatorship is not made merely for the purpose of repelling a foreign invasion or putting down the opposing groups. Rather he wants a dictatorship in order that he may use terror to force upon the country his own principles of morality. He says that this act is only to be a temporary measure preceding a new constitution. But in reality, he desires nothing short of using terror to extinguish from France *selfishness, honour, customs, manners, fashion, vanity, love of money, good companionship, intrigue, wit, sensuousness, and poverty*. Not until he, Robespierre, shall have accomplished these *miracles*, as he so rightly calls them, will he permit the law to reign again.[7]

The indirect approach to despotism

Usually, however, these gentlemen – the reformers, the legislators,

---

7   At this point in the original French text, Mr Bastiat pauses and speaks thus to all do-gooders and would-be rulers of mankind: 'Ah, you miserable creatures! You who think that you are so great! You who judge humanity to be so small! You who wish to reform everything! Why don't you reform yourselves? That task would be sufficient enough.'

and the writers on public affairs do not desire to impose direct despotism upon mankind. Oh no, they are too moderate and philanthropic for such direct action. Instead, they turn to the law for this despotism, this absolutism, this omnipotence. They desire only to make the laws.

To show the prevalence of this queer idea in France, I would need to copy not only the entire works of Mably, Raynal, Rousseau, and Fenelon – plus long extracts from Bossuet and Montesquieu – but also the entire proceedings of the Convention. I shall do no such thing; I merely refer the reader to them.

Napoleon wanted passive mankind

It is, of course, not at all surprising that this same idea should have greatly appealed to Napoleon. He embraced it ardently and used it with vigour. Like a chemist, Napoleon considered all Europe to be material for his experiments. But, in due course, this material reacted against him.

At St Helena, Napoleon – greatly disillusioned – seemed to recognise some initiative in mankind. Recognising this, he became less hostile to liberty. Nevertheless, this did not prevent him from leaving this lesson to his son in his will: 'To govern is to increase and spread morality, education, and happiness.'

After all this, it is hardly necessary to quote the same opinions from Morelly, Babeuf, Owen, Saint-Simon, and Fourier. Here are, however, a few extracts from Louis Blanc's book on the organisation of labour: 'In our plan, society receives its momentum from power.'

Now consider this: the impulse behind this momentum is to be supplied by the *plan* of Louis Blanc; his plan is to be forced upon society; the society referred to is the human race. Thus the human race is to receive its momentum from Louis Blanc.

Now it will be said that the people are free to accept or to reject this plan. Admittedly, people are free to accept or to reject *advice* from whomever they wish. But this is not the way in which Mr Louis Blanc understands the matter. He expects that his plan will be legalised, and thus forcibly imposed upon the people by the power of the law:

> In our plan, the state has only to pass labour laws (nothing else?) by means of which industrial progress can and must proceed *in complete liberty*. The state merely places society on an incline (that is all?). Then society will slide down this incline by the mere force of things, and by the natural workings of the *established mechanism*.

But what is this incline that is indicated by Mr Louis Blanc? Does it not lead to an abyss? (No, it leads to happiness.) If this is true, then why does not society go there of its own choice? (Because society does not know what it wants; it must be propelled.) What is to propel it? (Power.) And who is to supply the impulse for this power? (Why, the inventor of the machine – in this instance, Mr Louis Blanc.)

The vicious circle of socialism

We shall never escape from this circle: the idea of passive mankind, and the power of the law being used by a great man to propel the people.

Once on this incline, will society enjoy some liberty? (Certainly.) And what is liberty, Mr Louis Blanc?

> Once and for all, liberty is not only a mere granted right; it is

also the power granted to a person to use and to develop his faculties under a reign of justice and under the protection of the law.

And this is no pointless distinction; its meaning is deep and its consequences are difficult to estimate. For once it is agreed that a person, to be truly free, must have the power to use and develop his faculties, then it follows that every person has a claim on society for such education as will *permit him* to develop himself. It also follows that every person has a claim on society for tools of production, without which human activity cannot be fully effective. Now by what action can society give to every person the necessary education and the necessary tools of production, if not by the action of the state?

Thus, again, liberty is power. Of what does this power consist? (Of being educated and of being given the tools of production.) Who is to give the education and the tools of production? (Society, *which owes them to everyone*.) By what action is society to give tools of production to those who do not own them? (Why, *by the action of the state*.) And from whom will the state take them?

Let the reader answer that question. Let him also notice the direction in which this is taking us.

The doctrine of the democrats

The strange phenomenon of our times – one which will probably astound our descendants – is the doctrine based on this triple hypothesis: the total inertness of mankind, the omnipotence of the law, and the infallibility of the legislator. These three ideas form the sacred symbol of those who proclaim themselves totally democratic.

The advocates of this doctrine also profess to be *social*. So far as they are democratic, they place unlimited faith in mankind. But so far as they are social, they regard mankind as little better than mud. Let us examine this contrast in greater detail.

What is the attitude of the democrat when political rights are under discussion? How does he regard the people when a legislator is to be chosen? Ah, then it is claimed that the people have an instinctive wisdom; they are gifted with the finest perception; *their will is always right*; the general will *cannot err*; voting cannot be too universal. When it is time to vote, apparently the voter is not to be asked for any guarantee of his wisdom. His will and capacity to choose wisely are taken for granted. Can the people be mistaken? Are we not living in an age of enlightenment? What! are the people always to be kept on leashes? Have they not won their rights by great effort and sacrifice? Have they not given ample proof of their intelligence and wisdom? Are they not adults? Are they not capable of judging for themselves? Do they not know what is best for themselves? Is there a class or a man who would be so bold as to set himself above the people, and judge and act for them? No, no, the people are and should be *free*. They desire to manage their own affairs, and they shall do so.

But when the legislator is finally elected – ah! then indeed does the tone of his speech undergo a radical change. The people are returned to passiveness, inertness, and unconsciousness; the legislator enters into omnipotence. Now it is for him to initiate, to direct, to propel, and to organise. Mankind has only to submit; the hour of despotism has struck. We now observe this fatal idea: the people who, during the election, were so wise, so moral, and so perfect, now have no tendencies whatever; or if they have any, they are tendencies that lead downward into degradation.

The socialist concept of liberty

But ought not the people be given a little liberty?

But Mr Considerant has assured us that *liberty leads inevitably to monopoly!*

We understand that liberty means competition. But according to Mr Louis Blanc, competition is a system that ruins the businessmen and exterminates the people. It is for this reason that free people are ruined and exterminated in proportion to their degree of freedom. (Possibly Mr Louis Blanc should observe the results of competition in, for example, Switzerland, Holland, England, and the United States.)

Mr Louis Blanc also tells us that *competition leads to monopoly*. And by the same reasoning, he thus informs us that *low prices lead to high prices*; that *competition drives production to destructive activity*; that *competition drains away the sources of purchasing power*; that *competition forces an increase in production while, at the same time, it forces a decrease in consumption*. From this, it follows that free people produce for the sake of not consuming; that liberty means *oppression and madness* among the people; and that Mr Louis Blanc absolutely must attend to it.

Socialists fear all liberties

Well, what liberty should the legislators permit people to have? Liberty of conscience? (But if this were permitted, we would see the people taking this opportunity to become atheists.)

Then liberty of education? (But parents would pay professors to teach their children immorality and falsehoods; besides, according to Mr Thiers, if education were left to national liberty, it would cease to be national, and we would be teaching our children the ideas of the Turks or Hindus; whereas, thanks to this legal despotism over education, our children now have the good fortune to be taught the noble ideas of the Romans.)

Then liberty of labour? (But that would mean competition which, in turn, leaves production unconsumed, ruins businessmen, and exterminates the people.)

Perhaps liberty of trade? (But everyone knows – and the advocates of protective tariffs have proved over and over again – that freedom of trade ruins every person who engages in it, and that it is necessary to suppress freedom of trade in order to prosper.)

Possibly, then, liberty of association? (But, according to socialist doctrine, true liberty and voluntary association are in contradiction to each other, and the purpose of the socialists is to suppress liberty of association precisely in order to force people to associate together in true liberty.)

Clearly, then, the conscience of the social democrats cannot permit persons to have any liberty because they believe that the nature of mankind tends always towards every kind of degradation and disaster. Thus, of course, the legislators must make plans for the people in order to save them from themselves.

This line of reasoning brings us to a challenging question: if people are as incapable, as immoral, and as ignorant as the politicians indicate, then why is the right of these same people to vote defended with such passionate insistence?

The superman idea

The claims of these organisers of humanity raise another question which I have often asked them and which, so far as I know, they have never answered: if the natural tendencies of mankind are so bad that it is not safe to permit people to be free, how is it that the tendencies of these organisers are always good? Do not the legislators and their appointed agents also belong to the human race? Or do they believe that they themselves are made of a finer clay than the rest of mankind? The organisers maintain that society, when left undirected, rushes headlong to its inevitable destruction because the instincts of the people are so perverse. The legislators claim to stop this suicidal course and to give it a saner direction. Apparently, then, the legislators and the organisers have received from Heaven an intelligence and virtue that place them beyond and above mankind; if so, let them show their titles to this superiority.

They would be the shepherds over us, their sheep. Certainly such an arrangement presupposes that they are naturally superior to the rest of us. And certainly we are fully justified in demanding from the legislators and organisers proof of this natural superiority.

The socialists reject free choice

Please understand that I do not dispute their right to invent social combinations, to advertise them, to advocate them, and to try them upon themselves, at their own expense and risk. But I do dispute their right to impose these plans upon us by law – by force – and to compel us to pay for them with our taxes.

I do not insist that the supporters of these various social schools of thought – the Proudhonists, the Cabetists, the Fourierists, the Universitarists, and the Protectionists – renounce their various ideas. I insist only that they renounce this one idea that they have in common: they need only to give up the idea of *forcing* us to acquiesce to their groups and series, their socialised projects, their free-credit banks, their Graeco-Roman concept of morality, and their commercial regulations. I ask only that we be permitted to decide upon these plans for ourselves; that we not be forced to accept them, directly or indirectly, if we find them to be contrary to our best interests or repugnant to our consciences.

But these organisers desire access to the tax funds and to the power of the law in order to carry out their plans. In addition to being oppressive and unjust, this desire also implies the fatal supposition that the organiser is infallible and mankind is incompetent. But, again, if persons are incompetent to judge for themselves, then why all this talk about universal suffrage?

The cause of French revolutions

This contradiction in ideas is, unfortunately but logically, reflected in events in France. For example, Frenchmen have led all other Europeans in obtaining their rights – or, more accurately, their political demands. Yet this fact has in no respect prevented us from becoming the most governed, the most regulated, the most imposed upon, the most harnessed, and the most exploited people in Europe. France also leads all other nations as the one where revolutions are constantly to be anticipated. And under the circumstances, it is quite natural that this should be the case.

And this will remain the case so long as our politicians continue to accept this idea that has been so well expressed by Mr Louis Blanc: 'Society receives its momentum from power.' This will remain the case so long as human beings with feelings continue to remain passive; so long as they consider themselves incapable of bettering their prosperity and happiness by their own intelligence and their own energy; so long as they expect everything from the law; in short, so long as they imagine that their relationship to the state is the same as that of the sheep to the shepherd.

The enormous power of government

As long as these ideas prevail, it is clear that the responsibility of government is enormous. Good fortune and bad fortune, wealth and destitution, equality and inequality, virtue and vice – all then depend upon political administration. It is burdened with everything, it undertakes everything, it does everything; therefore it is responsible for everything.

If we are fortunate, then government has a claim to our gratitude; but if we are unfortunate, then government must bear the blame. For are not our persons and property now at the disposal of government? Is not the law omnipotent?

In creating a monopoly of education, the government must answer to the hopes of the fathers of families who have thus been deprived of their liberty; and if these hopes are shattered, whose fault is it?

In regulating industry, the government has contracted to make it prosper; otherwise it is absurd to deprive industry of its liberty. And if industry now suffers, whose fault is it?

In meddling with the balance of trade by playing with tariffs, the government thereby contracts to make trade prosper; and if this results in destruction instead of prosperity, whose fault is it?

In giving the maritime industries protection in exchange for their liberty, the government undertakes to make them profitable; and if they become a burden to the taxpayers, whose fault is it?

Thus there is not a grievance in the nation for which the

government does not voluntarily make itself responsible. Is it surprising, then, that every failure increases the threat of another revolution in France?

And what remedy is proposed for this? To extend indefinitely the domain of the law; that is, the responsibility of government.

But if the government undertakes to control and to raise wages, and cannot do it; if the government undertakes to care for all who may be in want, and cannot do it; if the government undertakes to support all unemployed workers, and cannot do it; if the government undertakes to lend interest-free money to all borrowers, and cannot do it; if, in these words that we regret to say escaped from the pen of Mr de Lamartine, 'The state considers that its purpose is to enlighten, to develop, to enlarge, to strengthen, to spiritualise, and to sanctify the soul of the people' – and if the government cannot do all of these things, what then? Is it not certain that after every government failure – which, alas!, is more than probable – there will be an equally inevitable revolution?

Politics and economics

[Now let us return to a subject that was briefly discussed in the opening pages of this thesis: the relationship of economics and of politics – political economy.[8]]

A science of economics must be developed before a science of politics can be logically formulated. Essentially, economics is the science of determining whether the interests of human beings are harmonious or antagonistic. This must be known before a science

---

8   Translator's note: Mr Bastiat has devoted three other books and several articles to the development of the ideas contained in the three sentences of the following paragraph.

of politics can be formulated to determine the proper functions of government.

Immediately following the development of a science of economics, and at the very beginning of the formulation of a science of politics, this all-important question must be answered: what is law? What ought it to be? What is its scope; its limits? Logically, at what point do the just powers of the legislator stop?

I do not hesitate to answer: *law is the common force organised to act as an obstacle to injustice*. In short, *law is justice*.

Proper legislative functions

It is not true that the legislator has absolute power over our persons and property. The existence of persons and property preceded the existence of the legislator, and his function is only to guarantee their safety.

It is not true that the function of law is to regulate our consciences, our ideas, our wills, our education, our opinions, our work, our trade, our talents, or our pleasures. The function of law is to protect the free exercise of these rights, and to prevent any person from interfering with the free exercise of these same rights by any other person.

Since law necessarily requires the support of force, its lawful domain is only in the areas where the use of force is necessary. This is justice.

Every individual has the right to use force for lawful self-defence. It is for this reason that the collective force – which is only the organised combination of the individual forces – may lawfully be used for the same purpose; and it cannot be used legitimately for any other purpose.

Law is solely the organisation of the individual right of self-defence which existed before law was formalised. Law is justice.

Law and charity are not the same

The mission of the law is *not* to oppress persons and plunder them of their property, even though the law may be acting in a philanthropic spirit. Its mission is to protect persons and property.

Furthermore, it must not be said that the law may be philanthropic if, in the process, it refrains from oppressing persons and plundering them of their property; this would be a contradiction. The law cannot avoid having an effect upon persons and property; and if the law acts in any manner except to protect them, its actions then necessarily violate the liberty of persons and their right to own property.

The law is justice – simple and clear, precise and bounded. Every eye can see it, and every mind can grasp it; for justice is measurable, immutable, and unchangeable. Justice is neither more than this nor less than this.

If you exceed this proper hmit – if you attempt to make the law religious, fraternal, equalising, philanthropic, industrial, literary, or artistic – you will then be lost in an uncharted territory, in vagueness and uncertainty, in a forced utopia or, even worse, in a multitude of utopias, each striving to seize the law and impose it upon you. This is true because fraternity and philanthropy, unlike justice, do not have precise limits. Once started, where will you stop? And where will the law stop itself?

The high road to communism

Mr de Saint-Cricq would extend his philanthropy only to some of the industrial groups; he would demand that the law *control the consumers to benefit the producers*.

Mr Considerant would sponsor the cause of the labour groups; he would use the law to secure for them *a guaranteed minimum of clothing, housing, food, and all other necessities of life*.

Mr Louis Blanc would say – and with reason – that these minimum guarantees are merely the beginning of complete fraternity; he would say that the law should give tools of production and free education to all working people.

Another person would observe that this arrangement would still leave room for inequality; he would claim that the law should give to everyone – even in the most inaccessible hamlet – luxury, literature, and art.

All of these proposals are the high road to communism; legislation will then be – in fact, it already is – the battlefield for the fantasies and greed of everyone.

The basis for stable government

Law is justice. In this proposition a simple and enduring government can be conceived. And I defy anyone to say how even the thought of revolution, of insurrection, of the slightest uprising could arise against a government whose organised force was confined only to suppressing injustice.

Under such a regime, there would be the most prosperity – and it would be the most equally distributed. As for the sufferings that are inseparable from humanity, none would even think of blaming the government for them. This is true because, if the force of government were limited to suppressing injustice, then government would be as innocent of these sufferings as it is now innocent of changes in the temperature.

As proof of this statement, consider this question: have the people ever been known to rise against the Court of Appeals, or mob a Justice of the Peace, in order to get higher wages, free credit, tools of production, favourable tariffs, or government-created jobs? Everyone knows perfectly well that such matters are not within the jurisdiction of the Court of Appeals or a Justice of the Peace. And if government were limited to its proper functions, everyone would soon learn that these matters are not within the jurisdiction of the law itself.

But make the laws upon the principle of fraternity – proclaim that all good, and all bad, stem from the law; that the law is responsible for all individual misfortunes and all social inequalities – then the door is open to an endless succession of complaints, irritations, troubles, and revolutions.

Justice means equal rights

Law is justice. And it would indeed be strange if law could properly be anything else! Is not justice right? Are not rights equal? By what right does the law force me to conform to the social plans of Mr Mimerel, Mr de Melun, Mr Thiers, or Mr Louis Blanc? If the law has a moral right to do this, why does it not, then, force these gentlemen to submit to *my plans*? Is it logical to suppose that nature has not given me sufficient imagination to dream up a utopia also? Should the law choose one fantasy among many, and put the organised force of government at its service only?

Law is justice. And let it not be said – as it continually is said –

that under this concept the law would be atheistic, individualistic, and heartless; that it would make mankind in its own image. This is an absurd conclusion, worthy only of those worshippers of government who believe that the law *is* mankind.

Nonsense! Do those worshippers of government believe that free persons will cease to act? Does it follow that if we receive no energy from the law, we shall receive no energy at all? Does it follow that if the law is restricted to the function of protecting the free use of our faculties, we will be unable to use our faculties? Suppose that the law does not force us to follow certain forms of religion, or systems of association, or methods of education, or regulations of labour, or regulations of trade, or plans for charity; does it then follow that we shall eagerly plunge into atheism, hermitary, ignorance, misery, and greed? If we are free, does it follow that we shall no longer recognise the power and goodness of God? Does it follow that we shall then cease to associate with each other, to help each other, to love and succour our unfortunate brothers, to study the secrets of nature, and to strive to improve ourselves to the best of our abilities?

The path to dignity and progress

Law is justice. And it is under the law of justice – under the reign of right; under the influence of liberty, safety, stability, and responsibility – that every person will attain his real worth and the true dignity of his being. It is only under this law of justice that mankind will achieve – slowly, no doubt, but certainly – God's design for the orderly and peaceful progress of humanity.

It seems to me that this is theoretically right, for whatever the question under discussion – whether religious, philosophical, political, or economic; whether it concerns prosperity, morality, equality, right, justice, progress, responsibility, cooperation, property, labour, trade, capital, wages, taxes, population, finance, or government – at whatever point on the scientific horizon I begin my researches, I invariably reach this one conclusion: the solution to the problems of human relationships is to be found in liberty.

Proof of an idea

And does not experience prove this? Look at the entire world. Which countries contain the most peaceful, the most moral, and the happiest people? Those people are found in the countries where the law least interferes with private affairs; where government is least felt; where the individual has the greatest scope, and free opinion the greatest influence; where administrative powers are fewest and simplest; where taxes are lightest and most nearly equal, and popular discontent the least excited and the least justifiable; where individuals and groups most actively assume their responsibilities, and, consequently, where the morals of admittedly imperfect human beings are constantly improving; where trade, assemblies, and associations are the least restricted; where labour, capital, and populations suffer the fewest forced displacements; where mankind most nearly follows its own natural inclinations; where the inventions of men are most nearly in harmony with the laws of God; in short, the happiest, most moral, and most peaceful people are those who most nearly follow this principle: although mankind is not perfect, still, all hope rests upon the free and voluntary actions of persons within the limits of right; law or force is to be used for nothing except the administration of universal justice.

The desire to rule over others

This must be said: there are too many 'great' men in the world – legislators, organisers, do-gooders, leaders of the people, fathers of nations, and so on, and so on. Too many persons place themselves above mankind; they make a career of organising it, patronising it, and ruling it.

Now someone will say: 'You yourself are doing this very thing.'

True. But it must be admitted that I act in an entirely different sense; if I have joined the ranks of the reformers, it is solely for the purpose of persuading them to leave people alone. I do not look upon people as Vancauson looked upon his automaton. Rather, just as the physiologist accepts the human body as it is, so do I accept people as they are. I desire only to study and admire.

My attitude towards all other persons is well illustrated by this story from a celebrated traveller: he arrived one day in the midst of a tribe of savages, where a child had just been born. A crowd of soothsayers, magicians, and quacks – armed with rings, hooks, and cords – surrounded it. One said: 'This child will never smell the perfume of a peace-pipe unless I stretch his nostrils.' Another said: 'He will never be able to hear unless I draw his ear-lobes down to his shoulders.' A third said: 'He will never see the sunshine unless I slant his eyes.' Another said: 'He will never stand upright unless I bend his legs.' A fifth said: 'He will never learn to think unless I flatten his skull.'

'Stop,' cried the traveller. 'What God does is well done. Do not claim to know more than He. God has given organs to this frail creature; let them develop and grow strong by exercise, use, experience, and liberty.'

Let us now try liberty

God has given to men all that is necessary for them to accomplish their destinies. He has provided a social form as well as a human form. And these social organs of persons are so constituted that they will develop themselves harmoniously in the clean air of liberty. Away, then, with quacks and organisers! Away with their rings, chains, hooks, and pincers! Away with their artificial systems! Away with the whims of governmental administrators, their socialised projects, their centralisation, their tariffs, their government schools, their state religions, their free credit, their bank monopolies, their regulations, their restrictions, their equalisation by taxation, and their pious moralisations!

And now that the legislators and do-gooders have so futilely inflicted so many systems upon society, may they finally end where they should have begun: may they reject all systems, and try liberty; for liberty is an acknowledgment of faith in God and His works.

ABOUT THE IEA

The Institute is a research and educational charity (No. CC 235 351), limited by guarantee. Its mission is to improve understanding of the fundamental institutions of a free society by analysing and expounding the role of markets in solving economic and social problems.

The IEA achieves its mission by:

- a high-quality publishing programme
- conferences, seminars, lectures and other events
- outreach to school and college students
- brokering media introductions and appearances

The IEA, which was established in 1955 by the late Sir Antony Fisher, is an educational charity, not a political organisation. It is independent of any political party or group and does not carry on activities intended to affect support for any political party or candidate in any election or referendum, or at any other time. It is financed by sales of publications, conference fees and voluntary donations.

In addition to its main series of publications the IEA also publishes a quarterly journal, *Economic Affairs*.

The IEA is aided in its work by a distinguished international Academic Advisory Council and an eminent panel of Honorary Fellows. Together with other academics, they review prospective IEA publications, their comments being passed on anonymously to authors. All IEA papers are therefore subject to the same rigorous independent refereeing process as used by leading academic journals.

IEA publications enjoy widespread classroom use and course adoptions in schools and universities. They are also sold throughout the world and often translated/reprinted.

Since 1974 the IEA has helped to create a worldwide network of 100 similar institutions in over 70 countries. They are all independent but share the IEA's mission.

Views expressed in the IEA's publications are those of the authors, not those of the Institute (which has no corporate view), its Managing Trustees, Academic Advisory Council members or senior staff.

Members of the Institute's Academic Advisory Council, Honorary Fellows, Trustees and Staff are listed on the following page.

The Institute of Economic Affairs
2 Lord North Street, Westminster, London SW1P 3LB
Tel: 020 7799 8900
Fax: 020 7799 2137
Email: iea@iea.org.uk
Internet: iea.org.uk

87

Other papers recently published by the IEA include:

A Market in Airport Slots
Keith Boyfield (editor), David Starkie, Tom Bass & Barry Humphreys
Readings 56; ISBN 0 255 36505 5; £10.00

Money, Inflation and the Constitutional Position of the Central Bank
Milton Friedman & Charles A. E. Goodhart
Readings 57; ISBN 0 255 36538 1; £10.00

railway.com
Parallels between the Early British Railways and the ICT Revolution
Robert C. B. Miller
Research Monograph 57; ISBN 0 255 36534 9; £12.50

The Regulation of Financial Markets
Edited by Philip Booth & David Currie
Readings 58; ISBN 0 255 36551 9; £12.50

Climate Alarmism Reconsidered
Robert L. Bradley Jr
Hobart Paper 146; ISBN 0 255 36541 1; £12.50

Government Failure: E. G. West on Education
Edited by James Tooley & James Stanfield
Occasional Paper 130; ISBN 0 255 36552 7; £12.50

Corporate Governance: Accountability in the?Marketplace
Elaine Sternberg
Second edition
Hobart Paper 147; ISBN 0 255 36542 x; £12.50

The Land Use Planning System
Evaluating Options for Reform
John Corkindale
Hobart Paper 148; ISBN 0 255 36550 0; £10.00

Economy and Virtue
Essays on the Theme of Markets and Morality
Edited by Dennis O'Keeffe
Readings 59; ISBN 0 255 36504 7; £12.50

Free Markets Under Siege
Cartels, Politics and Social Welfare
Richard A. Epstein
Occasional Paper 132; ISBN 0 255 36553 5; £10.00

Unshackling Accountants
D. R. Myddelton
Hobart Paper 149; ISBN 0 255 36559 4; £12.50

The Euro as Politics
Pedro Schwartz
Research Monograph 58; ISBN 0 255 36535 7; £12.50

Pricing Our Roads
Vision and Reality
Stephen Glaister & Daniel J. Graham
Research Monograph 59; ISBN 0 255 36562 4; £10.00

The Role of Business in the Modern World
Progress, Pressures, and Prospects for the Market Economy
David Henderson
Hobart Paper 150; ISBN 0 255 36548 9; £12.50

The Dangers of Bus Re-regulation

and Other Perspectives on Markets in Transport

John Hibbs et al.

Occasional Paper 137; ISBN 0 255 36572 1; £10.00

The New Rural Economy

Change, Dynamism and Government Policy

Berkeley Hill et al.

Occasional Paper 138; ISBN 0 255 36546 2; £15.00

The Benefits of Tax Competition

Richard Teather

Hobart Paper 153; ISBN 0 255 36569 1; £12.50

Wheels of Fortune

Self-funding Infrastructure and the Free Market Case for a Land Tax

Fred Harrison

Hobart Paper 154; ISBN 0 255 36589 6; £12.50

Were 364 Economists All Wrong?

Edited by Philip Booth

Readings 60; ISBN 978 0 255 36588 8; £10.00

Europe After the 'No' Votes

Mapping a New Economic Path

Patrick A. Messerlin

Occasional Paper 139; ISBN 978 0 255 36580 2; £10.00

The Railways, the Market and the Government

John Hibbs et al.

Readings 61; ISBN 978 0 255 36567 3; £12.50

Corruption: The World's Big C

Cases, Causes, Consequences, Cures

Ian Senior

Research Monograph 61; ISBN 978 0 255 36571 0; £12.50

Choice and the End of Social Housing

Peter King

Hobart Paper 155; ISBN 978 0 255 36568 0; £10.00

Sir Humphrey's Legacy

Facing Up to the Cost of Public Sector Pensions

Neil Record

Hobart Paper 156; ISBN 978 0 255 36578 9; £10.00

The Economics of Law

Cento Veljanovski

Second edition

Hobart Paper 157; ISBN 978 0 255 36561 1; £12.50

Living with Leviathan

Public Spending, Taxes and Economic Performance

David B. Smith

Hobart Paper 158; ISBN 978 0 255 36579 6; £12.50

The Vote Motive

Gordon Tullock

New edition

Hobart Paperback 33; ISBN 978 0 255 36577 2; £10.00

Waging the War of Ideas

John Blundell

Third edition

Occasional Paper 131; ISBN 978 0 255 36606 9; £12.50

The War Between the State and the Family
How Government Divides and Impoverishes
Patricia Morgan
Hobart Paper 159; ISBN 978 0 255 36596 3; £10.00

Capitalism – A Condensed Version
Arthur Seldon
Occasional Paper 140; ISBN 978 0 255 36598 7; £7.50

Catholic Social Teaching and the Market Economy
Edited by Philip Booth
Hobart Paperback 34; ISBN 978 0 255 36581 9; £15.00

Adam Smith – A Primer
Eamonn Butler
Occasional Paper 141; ISBN 978 0 255 36608 3; £7.50

Happiness, Economics and Public Policy
Helen Johns & Paul Ormerod
Research Monograph 62; ISBN 978 0 255 36600 7; £10.00

They Meant Well
Government Project Disasters
D. R. Myddelton
Hobart Paper 160; ISBN 978 0 255 36601 4; £12.50

Rescuing Social Capital from Social Democracy
John Meadowcroft & Mark Pennington
Hobart Paper 161; ISBN 978 0 255 36592 5; £10.00

Paths to Property
Approaches to Institutional Change in International Development
Karol Boudreaux & Paul Dragos Aligica
Hobart Paper 162; ISBN 978 0 255 36582 6; £10.00

Prohibitions

Edited by John Meadowcroft

Hobart Paperback 35; ISBN 978 0 255 36585 7; £15.00

Trade Policy, New Century

The WTO, FTAs and Asia Rising

Razeen Sally

Hobart Paper 163; ISBN 978 0 255 36544 4; £12.50

Sixty Years On – Who Cares for the NHS?

Helen Evans

Research Monograph 63; ISBN 978 0 255 36611 3; £10.00

Taming Leviathan

Waging the War of Ideas Around the World

Edited by Colleen Dyble

Occasional Paper 142; ISBN 978 0 255 36607 6; £12.50

The Legal Foundations of Free Markets

Edited by Stephen F. Copp

Hobart Paperback 36; ISBN 978 0 255 36591 8; £15.00

Climate Change Policy: Challenging the Activists

Edited by Colin Robinson

Readings 62; ISBN 978 0 255 36595 6; £10.00

Should We Mind the Gap?

Gender Pay Differentials and Public Policy

J. R. Shackleton

Hobart Paper 164; ISBN 978 0 255 36604 5; £10.00

Pension Provision: Government Failure Around the World

Edited by Philip Booth et al.

Readings 63; ISBN 978 0 255 36602 1; £15.00

New Europe's Old Regions

Piotr Zientara

Hobart Paper 165; ISBN 978 0 255 36617 5; £12.50

Central Banking in a Free Society

Tim Congdon

Hobart Paper 166; ISBN 978 0 255 36623 6; £12.50

The European Institutions as an Interest Group

Roland Vaubel

Hobart Paper 167; ISBN 978 0 255 36634 2; £10.00

Other IEA publications

Comprehensive information on other publications and the wider work of the IEA can be found at www.iea.org.uk. To order any publication please see below.

Personal customers

Orders from personal customers should be directed to the IEA:
Bob Layson
IEA
2 Lord North Street
FREEPOST LON10168
London SW1P 3YZ
Tel: 020 7799 8909. Fax: 020 7799 2137
Email: blayson@iea.org.uk

Trade customers

All orders from the book trade should be directed to the IEA's distributor:
Gazelle Book Services Ltd (IEA Orders)
FREEPOST RLYS-EAHU-YSCZ
White Cross Mills
Hightown
Lancaster LA1 4XS
Tel: 01524 68765, Fax: 01524 53232
Email: sales@gazellebooks.co.uk

IEA subscriptions

The IEA also offers a subscription service to its publications. For a single annual payment (currently £42.00 in the UK), subscribers receive every monograph the IEA publishes. For more information please contact:
Adam Myers
Subscriptions
IEA
2 Lord North Street
FREEPOST LON10168
London SW1P 3YZ
Tel: 020 7799 8920, Fax: 020 7799 2137
Email: amyers@iea.org.uk